D1172223

BETTER BOARDROOMS

Repairing Corporate Governance
for the 21st Century

ALSO BY PATRICIA MEREDITH

Catalytic Governance: Leading Change in the Information Age, by Patricia Meredith, Steven A. Rosell, and Ged R. Davis (Rotman-UTP Publishing, an imprint of University of Toronto Press, 2016)

Stumbling Giants: Transforming Canada's Banks for the Information Age, by Patricia Meredith and James L. Darroch (Rotman-UTP Publishing, an imprint of University of Toronto Press, 2017)

BETTER
BOARDROOMS

Repairing Corporate Governance
for the 21st Century

PATRICIA MEREDITH

UNIVERSITY OF TORONTO PRESS
Toronto Buffalo London

Rotman-UTP Publishing
An imprint of University of Toronto Press
Toronto Buffalo London
utorontopress.com

© Patricia Meredith 2020

Library and Archives Canada Cataloguing in Publication

Title: Better boardrooms : repairing corporate governance for the
   21st century / Patricia Meredith.
Names: Meredith, Patricia, 1955–, author.
Description: Includes bibliographical references and index.
Identifiers: Canadiana (print) 20200307363 | Canadiana (ebook) 20200307460 |
   ISBN 9781442649750 (hardcover) | ISBN 9781442621381 (EPUB) |
   ISBN 9781442621374 (PDF)
Subjects: LCSH: Corporate governance – Canada. | LCSH: Bank directors –
   Canada. | LCSH: Banks and banking – Canada.
Classification: LCC HG1616.D5 M47 2020 | DDC 332.1068/40971 – dc23

ISBN 978-1-4426-4975-0 (cloth)   ISBN 978-1-4426-2138-1 (EPUB)
                               ISBN 978-1-4426-2137-4 (PDF)

Printed in Canada

We acknowledge the financial support of the Government of Canada, the Canada Council for the Arts, and the Ontario Arts Council, an agency of the Government of Ontario, for our publishing activities.

Canada Council   Conseil des Arts
for the Arts   du Canada

ONTARIO ARTS COUNCIL
CONSEIL DES ARTS DE L'ONTARIO
an Ontario government agency
un organisme du gouvernement de l'Ontario

Funded by the Financé par le
Government gouvernement
of Canada   du Canada   Canadä

MIX
Paper from
responsible sources
FSC FSC® C016245

This book is dedicated to four men who have helped me identify and interpret disruptive change; apply strategy and governance in a rapidly changing environment; make sense of what I observed in the corporate arena; and understand the implications for governance in the information age.

James Williams,
founder and president,
Williams Inference Global
(died in 2010)

Allan L. (Al) Flood,
former chairman and chief executive officer,
Canadian Imperial Bank of Commerce

Michael C. Jensen,
Jesse Isidor Straus professor of business administration,
Harvard Business School

Steven A. Rosell,
president,
Viewpoint Learning
(died in 2018)

Contents

Preface: What Got Me Started ...

This is the third book in a trilogy. The first volume, *Catalytic Governance: Leading Change in the Information Age*, co-authored with Steven Rosell and Ged Davis, set out a process for leading transformative change. It was based on our experience with the Canadian Task Force for the Payments System Review. The second book, *Stumbling Giants: Transforming Canada's Banks for the Information Age*, co-authored with James Darroch, examined how poorly positioned the Canadian banks are to withstand the social and technological tsunami sweeping over financial services. That book was primarily aimed at the enthusiastic young bankers who realize that their industry must change if it is to regain its reputation as a vibrant enabler of economic growth. But, as James and I made clear, the dreams of these men and women will not be realized unless a broad cross-section of Canadians – policy makers and regulators, customers, suppliers, investors, and, not least, the bankers themselves – work together to create a banking system better suited to the twenty-first century.

This, my third book, covers a much bigger and more pressing challenge: the need for a new system of corporate governance that takes account of the fast-changing business environment. The shortcomings of our present governance system have been on my mind ever since I became head of corporate strategy at Canadian Imperial

Bank of Commerce, in 1993. I thought I had come up with some answers ten years ago, when I wrote my PhD dissertation on the impact of disruptive change on the residential mortgage industry, but my ideas turned out to be based more on hope than on reality. My view was that companies did not respond to disruptive change because they failed to see the longer-term implications of what was going on around them, and because conflicts of interest and inertia got in the way of real change. In a nutshell, as a former Canadian bank CEO said to me after a friendly discussion about trends in the financial services industry, "It isn't going to happen on my watch, and I am not going to do anything about it." It became clear to me that if the chief executive would not do anything to fix a broken system, neither would anyone else, including the board of directors.

I have been working on strategy, uncertainty, and governance for twenty-five years, yet I am only now starting to fully grasp the challenges of managing strategic risk in the information age. Much of my initial thinking was based on my experience with public, private, and not-for-profit boards. But the traditional approach has failed dismally, as most incumbents struggle to compete effectively against upstart rivals in an entirely new environment – the information age, marked by a seismic shift from traditional industries spawned by the Industrial Revolution to an economy based on data. The information-age model is based on a commodity that is quickly and widely disseminated using computing and communications technology. Its hallmarks are high up-front investments in intangibles and very low reproduction costs, the inverse of the industrial age. As a result, the information economy requires entirely new governance processes that prioritize timely engagement, dialogue, and learning, rather than expert meetings long after the opportunity has presented itself.

At first, I thought that companies could avoid the tremendous loss of financial and human resources that takes place when they fail to adapt if only their boards of directors paid more attention to changes in the external environment, and then focused on turning those challenges into opportunities. Sadly, I've discovered that the conflicts of interest that confront corporate managers have also infiltrated the boardroom. The fact is that very few late-career executives or directors are brave enough to initiate transformative change. They would much prefer their company just to tread water until they retire, and to dump the problem in their successors' laps.

Four men have awakened me to the failure of existing governance structures to recognize and respond to the changes that are buffeting business, especially in North America and Britain.

I was fortunate to meet Jim Williams of Williams Inference Global in 1994. For more than forty years, Jim scanned newspapers and periodicals, finding investment ideas in hidden and unintended messages. He picked up the technique from Connecticut's Carniglia brothers: Ettore, a physician, and Francis, a veterinarian. From them he learned the fundamentals of sound diagnosis: keep an open mind, observe carefully, and let conclusions emerge. Jim's approach was to find anomalies, which according to American physicist, historian, and philosopher Thomas Kuhn, is the first step in recognizing a scientific revolution. Jim taught me to identify anomalies, watch if they form a pattern, and then draw inferences about their longer-term impact on a company or industry. He recognized the Internet's impact on business a decade before its widespread adoption. Running through his work is the message that recognizing disruptive change early is critical to a company's long-term well-being. Failing to do so is sure to lead to disaster.

Also in the 1990s, my then boss, Al Flood, CIBC's chief executive, told me, "Your job is strategy, governance, and advice if the business units ask for it." His instruction summarized the role of the bank's stewards – in our case, the newly created "corporate center" (which I will define in detail later in this book). It was clear to me that the board of directors did not have the resources, knowledge, or time to do this job properly. The bank had a stake in more than seventy different businesses, some of which were incredibly profitable while others were losing piles of money. Each of these businesses faced its own competitors and its own challenges, stemming from profound changes in technology, customer attitudes, and banking regulation. Getting to grips with each one required access to management information and an ability to untangle the true meaning for the business from the mass of regulation-driven financial reporting that the bank was required to churn out. Al Flood was a master at understanding and addressing business risk. By the time he retired in 1999, CIBC was recognized as Canada's most innovative bank and the one best positioned for the twenty-first century. Unfortunately, as I describe in the first chapter of this book, that potential was never realized.

Time and again, experts have sought to expose the shortcomings of existing corporate-governance models, but almost all of them have failed – with one notable exception. In 1999, I went to work with Michael C. Jensen, Harvard Business School's organizational strategy guru and a senior adviser at the Monitor Group consultancy. Michael's 1991 *Harvard Business Review* article "Eclipse of the Public Corporation" had a huge impact on my thinking. He argued that if directors were unable or unwilling to act as long-term stewards of their companies, then most businesses, especially public companies, would not survive disruptive changes, such as those ushered in by the Internet, the information-based economy, and the financial crises of 1998 and 2008. This argument made its mark on Mark Wiseman, former chief executive of the CPP Investment Board, Canada's biggest pension fund manager and former head of global equities for Blackrock, one of the world's biggest investment managers. For eight years, from 2010 to 2018, Mark and Dominic Barton, formerly McKinsey & Company's global managing partner and now Canada's ambassador to China, spent much of their time (though with limited success) trying to convince North American and European companies to focus on longer-term threats and opportunities.

In 2010, Canada's then finance minister, the late Jim Flaherty, asked me to chair a review of the country's payments system. This assignment brought me face-to-face with the scale of the governance challenge that the financial-services industry faces. The banks' hugely profitable payments-processing business was being threatened by innovative outsiders. These upstarts were not all that interested in processing payments; rather, they wanted access to the heap of data that accompanies every payment – what you buy, when and where you buy it, how you pay for it, what other items you look at before buying, and so on. They could use these details to fuel their *real* businesses, whether search engines, social media platforms, or other financial services. Google, Apple, Facebook, Amazon, Alibaba, Tencent, and a myriad of technology companies that deliver financial services, known as fintechs, are in the information business. These companies are very different from traditional banks in that most of them have few tangible assets and just a handful of employees. That means their costs are a tiny fraction of the banks' costs. Instead, their businesses are built around valuable customer data.

As I came face-to-face with the realization that the payments business was evolving into an information business with an entirely new business model, I realized that the traditional task-force approach to governance – conducting research, hearing stakeholder and expert opinions, and then making recommendations – would not be adequate to transform the Canadian payments system for the twenty-first century. So, I asked Steve Rosell of Viewpoint Learning to develop a process that would use dialogue as its guiding principle, enabling consumers, industry, governments, and businesses to work together on building the payments system Canada needs. To that end, our task force convened a "payments roundtable" from which a "coalition of the willing" emerged, ready and able to shape ideas that would take account of the fast-moving environment in the payments system. This coalition became the backbone of the payments self-governing body, and the model for our recommendations to the minister on governance of the industry. It affirmed that governance in the future was a process, not a hierarchical body. The task force then provided resources to help various working groups flesh out those ideas. What transpired over the next eighteen months was truly transformative. Mindsets shifted, mental maps were redrawn, and the payments industry started working cooperatively to take the Canadian payments system into the digital age.

Drawing on the success of this project, I joined forces with Steve Rosell and Ged Davis, an expert in scenario planning who worked with Steve on payments, to develop a coherent model for leading transformative change in the information age. That model was articulated in my first book, *Catalytic Governance*, in 2016. It uses dialogue to engage stakeholders, explore alternative perspectives, develop shared mental maps and a common vision of the future, and devise the strategies needed to bring those ideas to fruition.

Steve continues to have a profound impact on my thinking and writing. Having spent almost five decades questioning how organizations (including businesses) and societies learn, and how that affects the way we govern ourselves, Steve has given me an unrivalled insight into the challenge of leading and governing in the information age. He has stressed the critical importance of engagement, dialogue, and learning to effective governance in the information age. Many of the recommendations outlined in the final chapter of this book had their origin in our conversations.

The banks' obliviousness to the threat posed by fintechs to their traditional payments business was driven home to me again in 2017 when James Darroch and I sent copies of *Stumbling Giants* to the chairs of each of Canada's big six banks, with an offer to meet them for a chat on the new wave of competition threatening to engulf their institutions. Not one of them replied. On other fronts, too, the banks' actions have spoken louder than words. Instead of transforming themselves to compete with the fintechs, most have chosen to add another layer to their decades-old mainframe systems to give customers the appearance (but not the reality) of faster payment-processing times. This approach only postpones the inevitable by saddling the banks with a cost structure many times that of their nimbler rivals.

The book on the banks has given me a better understanding of just how dramatically different the information age is. Not only is it about disruptive technologies, such as the mobile Internet, artificial intelligence, quantum and cloud computing, robots, and 3D printing, it is also ushering in an entirely new economic model marked by high upfront costs and very low reproduction costs. This model conveys a great advantage to first movers, particularly if the technology becomes an industry standard. Value creation comes from investment in intangibles, mostly proprietary ideas and intellectual property. As Jonathan Haskel and Stian Westlake, authors of *Capitalism without Capital*, put it,

> Early in the twenty-first century a quiet revolution occurred. For the first time, the major developed economies began to invest more in intangible assets, like design, branding and software, than in tangible assets, like machinery, buildings, and computers. For all sorts of businesses, the ability to deploy assets that one can neither see nor touch is increasingly the main source of long-term success.[1]

This quiet revolution extends well beyond the economy. The impact of the information age on society at large is likely to be as great as or greater than that on the economy. An educated population with access to information and the ability to share their views on strategy and policy instantaneously will expect to have a much bigger say in governance, including corporate governance. Successful companies will have to create communities of interest, engage stakeholders in dialogue, and lay out their future direction supported by clearly articulated principles and beliefs. The board's role will be to ensure that the company is delivering on its promises and positioning itself for the future.

I continue to ask the following question: Why have boards of directors been so ineffective in dealing with the threats inherent in disruptive change? This book is my response to that question. My aim is to spur a public conversation on the board's role in corporate strategy and managing uncertainty, and to reduce the tremendous waste of resources – financial, human, intellectual, social, and environmental – that takes place when companies fail to respond effectively to external forces that are so obviously shaping their futures. More important, my goal is to help steer corporate governance toward a more inclusive and productive future.

It has been a long and arduous journey, but I am confident that we are now on the cusp of an exciting adventure. As the information age transforms business, the existing corporate governance model will have to change. Gone are the days of the vertically integrated hierarchical business dominated by a corporate titan (think Henry

Ford) and his (yes, almost always *his*) tightly controlled group of directors and senior executives isolated on the C-suite floor. Information-age companies are networks of independent contractors, partnerships both public and private, and a few employees bound together by a common vision and purpose. A more collaborative approach to governance that ensures stakeholders' voices are heard will be essential for survival. As the boundaries blur between industries, and as powerful new data-gathering tools give stakeholders access to much more information, there is no doubt that companies will need to work far more closely with policy makers, regulators, customers, suppliers, partners, and investors if they are to boost their returns, create sustainable businesses, and maintain their credibility. In short, corporate governance is set for a major overhaul. The sooner it happens, the better for all of us.

BETTER BOARDROOMS

Repairing Corporate Governance for the 21st Century

CHAPTER ONE

CIBC: A Fork in the Road

I will never forget the evening of Tuesday, 2 April 1999 – and nor should any director, employee, or shareholder, past or present, of the Canadian Imperial Bank of Commerce.

I had been working at CIBC since 1987, first as the financial services industry analyst at its securities arm, CIBC Wood Gundy, and then as chief strategy adviser to Al Flood, who took the reins as the bank's chairman and chief executive in 1992. Working at Al's side, I was fortunate to be privy for seven years to almost every major move that the bank's board and its senior managers contemplated. It was an exciting time as we grappled with the bankruptcy of Olympia & York Developments (CIBC was one of its biggest creditors), bank mergers, the early days of the Internet, and no end of other crises.[1]

After seven years in the hot seat, Al had let it be known that he was ready to retire, and the board of directors gathered that April spring day to choose his successor. Together with half a dozen senior colleagues, we waited nervously on the fifth floor of Commerce Court West, CIBC's head office on the corner of King and Bay Streets in Toronto, to hear the outcome of their deliberations.

CIBC was in good shape at that time. It was vying with Royal Bank of Canada to be the biggest of Canada's big five banks, measured by assets. It was blessed with a strong branch network, a talented and innovative management team, and a sturdy balance sheet, and its future looked bright. Most important, it had set up a branchless bank, Amicus, whose partnership with the Loblaw's supermarket chain and its President's Choice brand would give CIBC a springboard into the twenty-first century. The bank had also forged partnerships with Fiserv, a global financial services technology supplier, and with the Silicon Valley electronics pioneer Hewlett-Packard to help it make the transition from old mainframe computers to modern, Internet-based technology.

As the directors deliberated, it dawned on me that, with Al about to step down, the bank had arrived at a critical fork in its 132-year history. The question was: what direction would it take? The two candidates for the top job could not have been more different in their backgrounds, their skills, or their visions for the bank.

One, Holger Kluge, had come to Canada from his native Germany as a young boy after the Second World War. He joined the Canadian Imperial Bank after high school and worked his way up the ranks, finishing his commerce and MBA degrees at night school. Holger spent ten years building partnerships as CIBC's representative in Asia, including an especially important one with Li Ka-Shing, the Hong Kong-based tycoon who was CIBC's largest shareholder at that time. He then rose to executive vice-president of international operations and, in 1990, took the reins of CIBC's personal and commercial operations, charged with cleaning up its troublesome consumer-loan portfolio.[2]

By contrast, the second candidate, John Hunkin, came from a prominent Toronto family. John's father had been CIBC's general manager when the forceful Russell Harrison was at the helm in the late 1970s. John himself joined the Bank of Commerce as a corporate banker after completing an undergraduate economics degree and an MBA. In the early 1980s, he worked with Al Flood to set up the bank's office in New York, a time both he and Al recalled fondly. He then moved into investment banking and headed Wood Gundy after CIBC acquired it in 1988. Four years later, Al named John president of the newly combined investment and corporate banks.

If Holger was to get the nod for the top job, I was confident that the bank would gradually equip itself for the twenty-first century. Holger had made it clear that he planned to shift resources from corporate and investment banking into the retail and commercial side of the business. He would continue to transform the retail bank into three distinct segments – high-end customers, the mass market, and out-of-branch banking – while modernizing its technology infrastructure. His plan was to move cautiously but unmistakably forward, focused on CIBC's long-term competitiveness and prosperity. He sketched a future where retail business would make up 80 per cent of the bank, and wholesale just 20 per cent, versus 40 and 60 per cent, respectively, in the early 1990s. His view was that the wholesale business had been far too volatile over the previous two decades, with a crisis erupting every four or five years that wiped out all the wholesale bank's recent profits. Each time this happened, the board of directors and senior management had opted to postpone investments, especially in new technology, that would have ushered the retail bank towards a brighter and more secure future.

John, on the other hand, promised the board that his top priority would be to push the bank's share price up to $100 per share, more than three times higher than it was in 1999. That implied plowing more financial and human resources into corporate lending and investment banking, and the risks that went with these businesses.* It also meant handing a blank check to Amicus to expand its US presence by capturing as much market share as possible, profitable or not, while investors went crazy over these new online businesses.

The board took more than eight hours to make up its mind. It was shortly after five p.m. when Paul Fisher, the company secretary, walked onto the executive floor to tell us that John Hunkin would be our new boss. I was shocked that the board had chosen the

---

* Over the previous decade, capital markets had disintermediated the bank's best credits, leaving them with higher-risk loan portfolios.

much riskier corporate strategy over a slow and steady evolution into retail banking. I sensed immediately that the choice marked not only a turning point for CIBC but also, as we shall see in later chapters, the start of an object lesson in governance for all big North American corporations.

The contest between Holger and John for the top job turned out to be a rerun of Aesop's fable about the tortoise and the hare. The two men had been vying for the top job for seven years, ever since the day Al named his first senior management team.[3] John, the hare, was quick off the mark with a new strategy for his side of the business, the corporate and investment bank. It moved forward in fits and starts, depending on the vagaries of the market. It sometimes even seemed to go backward as he and his colleagues were forced to regroup after encountering unexpected obstacles, such as the 1997 Asian financial crisis that curtailed World Markets' global expansion. Holger, on the other hand, moved slowly and deliberately, taking two years to devise a retail banking strategy, which was then gradually rolled out across the country.

It struck me on that fateful evening in 1999 that the board had made a choice (whether consciously or not) to put short-term stock performance above long-term sustainability. The next five years would confirm those fears. In mid-1999, CIBC was vying with Royal Bank to be the country's largest and most innovative bank. Yet by the time John retired just six years later, CIBC was the smallest of the Big Five, and considered the most likely to walk into sharp objects.[4] The stagnation continued for ten more years after it fell to John's successor, the ultra-cautious Gerry McCaughey, to repair the damage.

Al Flood started working at CIBC fresh out of high school in 1951. By the time he became CEO, he knew what needed to be done to keep the bank abreast of the unfolding digital age. Near the top of the list was changing CIBC's stodgy culture. For example, he spearheaded a three-day workshop, *The Digital Tsunami*, to encourage one hundred executives and outside partners to test new ideas in the early days of Internet banking. Among those ideas were the President's Choice

Financial partnership with Loblaw Companies, the Amicus bank in the United States, and the Intria joint ventures. Most important, Al saw himself as a steward of CIBC's long-term well-being – in the form of its financial, human, customer, social, and physical resources – and he restructured the senior executive team to ensure that we all focused on the same goal.

When Al took over in 1992, the bank was recovering from a brush with disaster caused by its over-exposure to the real-estate market, notably Olympia & York.[5] He decided on a top-to-toe housecleaning, starting with the formation of a new campus that he called a "leadership center." The center, located in King City north of Toronto, was designed to encourage an acceptance of change among the bank's senior managers, a group infamously described by Al's predecessor, Donald Fullerton, as "middle management mush."[6] The leadership center offered programs to reinforce CIBC's business strategies and to involve management more effectively in their implementation. The workshops and courses were less about learning new skills than changing mindsets, sharing experiences, and exchanging information. Anyone who attended them knew that their old ways of doing things would be questioned, and that they would be probed, pushed, and tested to come up with fresh ideas.

With the help of the deliberations at the leadership center, Al and his team set about redefining CIBC's structure, vision, and values. The bank was split into two divisions – one focusing on corporate and investment business, the other on personal and commercial clients. The split recognized that the wholesale banking side was much further along in the transition from traditional banking – taking deposits and making loans – to an entirely new business model that provided loans in the form of securities backed by underlying assets, such as real estate, credit-card receivables, and motor vehicles. Al set five key measures of performance – customer service, risk, people management, financial results, and operational effectiveness. In each case, a senior executive reporting directly to the CEO was accountable for delivering results.

The corporate and investment arm, led by John Hunkin, unveiled its new strategy with much fanfare in 1993. It would set up client-service teams to take care of a customer's every need, instead of having different parts of the bank bombarding that customer with overlapping products. It would develop imaginative new risk-management tools, including derivatives to support both its own activities and its clients. It would expand globally – in the United States, London, and Singapore – to meet customers' needs around the world.

Alas, this strategy stalled quickly as it became clear that the management team was not prepared to drive through changes in one of Al's key measures of performance: their compensation. The idea was to overhaul the performance-evaluation system, from assessing individual contributions to specific transactions to the success of an entire client-service team. But the process became mired in complexity and was soon abandoned. Not surprisingly, employees quickly understood this to mean that nothing had really changed, and they continued to flog the products that paid them the most rather than working for the good of the team and the client. For the next seven years, the president of CIBC World Markets, the new name for the corporate and investment bank, talked up the client-driven strategy, but in reality, little had changed. CIBC World Markets was still Canadian Imperial Bank of Commerce and Wood Gundy, and it was still flogging products, wherever they could be found.

On the other hand, the retail bank, in line with Holger's personality, moved more cautiously but also more steadily. The transformation started in the early 1990s, when CIBC created a stand-alone credit-card unit to compete head-to-head with American Express and other new entrants from the United States such as MBNA and Capital One. Within five years, the bank had become the leading credit-card issuer in Canada. CIBC's Aerogold card, linked to Air Canada's Aeroplan loyalty program, dominated the upscale market with a return on capital of more than 75 per cent.

Under Holger's stewardship, the personal and commercial bank set up another stand-alone business focused on home mortgages.

Over the previous decade, the mortgage business had fragmented from a single, vertically integrated unit into half a dozen distinct segments, each with its own business model and competitors. Because CIBC lacked the skills and resources necessary to create a full-service "mortgage bank," it chose the acquisition route, buying the only such operation in Canada, FirstLine Trust. "Our mortgage strategy," the bank said in 1997, "is to build a best practice capability around each stage in the life of a mortgage – originations, servicing and portfolio management."[7] By 1999, CIBC was on the verge of overtaking Royal Bank as the largest home-mortgage lender in the country.

Holger also recognized that in the eyes of the customer there was little to distinguish one Canadian bank from another beyond the color of their logos. Each served its customers with basically the same products through branches in much the same locations. He decided to do things a little differently by splitting CIBC's retail operations into two new brands, named Convenience Banking and Imperial Service. The former focused on the mass market's everyday needs. Figuring that the vast majority of consumers need seven banking products at most, Holger dramatically culled CIBC's offerings, simplified pricing and processing, and reconfigured the bricks-and-mortar branches. Most of these customers' needs could easily be met through self-service channels – ATMs and telephone and online banking – freeing up valuable (and costly) staff for sales and service. The future of branches for mass-market banking was in doubt, so CIBC worked on a more flexible kiosk system for its bricks-and-mortar – or, to be more accurate, molded-plastic – network.

To test the kiosk concept, CIBC ran an experiment at fourteen branches in the Niagara region of Ontario in 1994. All teller counters were dismantled one weekend, and the ATMs were moved inside the branch. The tellers' main job was now to teach customers how to use the ATMs. Over the next three months the Niagara branches boosted the transactions performed by customers rather than tellers from around 65 per cent to well over 90 per cent. Customer satisfaction improved, and so did

Figure 1.1. Traditional Bank Structure

the bank's bottom line. Most important, however, such moves ushered CIBC into a new era, laying the foundation for solid long-term success.

Imperial Service, as the name suggested, was reserved for the bank's most prized customers – those with significant assets (or liabilities) and more complex needs. CIBC trained a fresh cadre of investment and credit specialists. It set up a wealth-management division that offered multiple options – mutual funds, discretionary asset management, discount and full-service securities brokerage, and so on. One in every five customers was moved from a branch to a "relationship manager," in recognition of the fact that this small group contributed almost all the retail bank's profits. CIBC is still the only Canadian bank that offers an integrated borrowing, investing, and payments service through a single relationship manager

But by early 1994, Al Flood had started to realize that the traditional bank structure (see figure 1.1) was creating friction between the wholesale and retail support groups, and thus between the two new banking divisions. Because their needs for human resources, risk management, information technology, finance, and legal were so different, it made more sense to give each of the two business units its own support teams. This in turn changed the role of CIBC's senior management team. Under the traditional structure, no one except the chief executive exercised oversight of the bank's seventy or so separate businesses. In theory, the board of directors should

Figure 1.2. Governance-Oriented Corporate Center

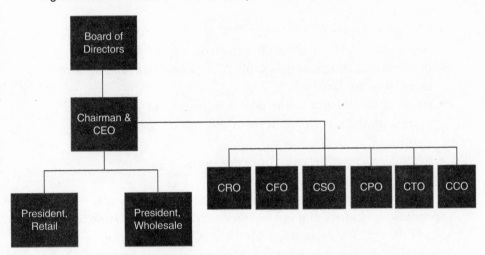

CRO = Chief Risk Officer; CFO = Chief Financial Officer; CSO = Chief Strategy Officer;
CPO = Chief People Officer; CTO = Chief Technology Officer; CCO = Chief Compliance Officer

also be a key part of such a structure, but in practice, as will become clear in later chapters, this is seldom the case.

Al Flood's new structure (figure 1.2) recognized that each business unit had different needs and that customers could be better served by decentralizing support functions, such as technology, human resources, risk management, and finance. Head office would concentrate on corporate strategy, policy, and governance. These changes were also meant to be a catalyst for developing an integrated strategic direction for the bank as a whole that each core business could not achieve on its own.

Most important, these changes meant a dramatic shift in CIBC's governance model, redefining the roles of senior management. Our job now was to:

- initiate and execute overall bank strategy. This included identifying new business opportunities; pursuing mergers, acquisitions, and divestitures; and building or buying the capabilities that we lacked;

- oversee business unit strategy. That involved providing governance and oversight through control of the planning process, performance monitoring, sector capital allocation, and appointment of sector heads;
- provide formal and informal mechanisms, such as the leadership center, which could form the "glue" for a uniform culture;
- exploit synergies between business units.

Al Flood unveiled the reorganization on 3 May 1994, and the new approach to strategy and governance was in place by October. First, head office staff was chopped from 13,000 to 2,000, mostly focusing on finance and risk management. Although many employees moved into the stand-alone business segments, most joined the bank's new joint ventures or left. Then, Al borrowed a page from Jack Welch's approach at General Electric and began reviewing each of the seventy or so businesses in the bank's portfolio. Using a model developed by Michael Porter, the Harvard Business School strategy guru, each business was asked to evaluate its competitive environment over the next five years. If it was not already number one or number two in its segment, it was told to draw up a plan to achieve that position. For those unable to come up with a convincing plan, the leadership team would examine other alternatives, including sale, joint venture, or closure.

One of the first units to feel the pressure was paper-based transaction processing. The Internet and process automation were rapidly making these activities redundant, which meant that the bank had a lot of money invested in soon-to-be-obsolete assets. After evaluating four potential partners, CIBC moved this business into a joint venture with Fiserv, a US company that provided back-office processing to more than 5,000 mid-sized American banks. Fiserv was far ahead of CIBC in applying technology to transaction processing, and with its help, CIBC slashed its processing costs in half over the next five years.

If paper processing was redundant, so too were large data-processing centers and mainframe computers. As a result, the bank formed another partnership, with Hewlett-Packard (HP). In what was the world's largest bank outsourcing arrangement to that time, HP managed all CIBC's PC, mainframe, and communications infrastructure.

Al Flood and his team applied the same logic to the corporate trust and custody business. A review showed that decades of underinvestment in technology made it impossible for this unit to meet customers' expectations, or to turn a profit. After evaluating four potential partners, we ended up folding them into a successful joint venture with US-based Mellon Bank, the world's third-largest provider of custody services.

Other laggards were simply put on the block. The equipment-leasing unit, known as Comcorp, was sold to CIT Group Inc. of New York, a specialist in commercial financing. The payroll-processing business went to Automatic Data Processing, a New Jersey-based provider of human-resources-management software and services. The bank's real-estate arm was scaled back to managing CIBC branches and offices. And so on. These disposals were a big deal, not just for CIBC but for the entire banking sector. Until then, it was virtually unheard of for a Canadian bank to turn its back on a sizable business.

In 1996, CIBC came close to merging the personal and commercial banking unit with Canada Trust, at the time the country's biggest trust company specializing in mass-market savings and mortgage lending. However, then Prime Minister Jean Chretien did not want news of a politically sensitive deal to emerge during that year's election campaign, and instructed his finance minister, Paul Martin, to turn down the acquisition. Had the merger gone through, the Canadian banking scene would look very different today. Not only would the deal have turned CIBC into the country's largest retail bank, but it would have given its retail business far more prominence: instead of 60 per cent of the bank's capital being tied up in wholesale operations and 40 per cent in retail, with the addition of Canada Trust those numbers would have been reversed. Al would thus have realized his goal of raising the profile of the more stable and profitable retail business. But it was not to be.[8]

Even so, the personal and commercial bank continued to move steadily ahead with its transformation, especially in the area of technology. Its most exciting initiative was a new "bank in a box," called Amicus. Using fledgling Internet technology and partnering with outside entrepreneurs, Amicus built an entirely new bank, which formed the nucleus of a partnership with Loblaw Companies to create President's Choice Financial, which opened its first kiosks in 1996.

President's Choice was truly a bank of the future. It did not have branches. Instead, it operated online and through kiosks in Loblaw supermarkets. It charged no transaction fees, paid higher interest on savings, and charged lower rates on loans than any other Canadian bank. Because it had no branches and relied on Loblaw's marketing to attract customers, its costs were less than half those of any other bank. And it passed much of these savings on to its customers. For the next two decades, President's Choice Financial and ING Direct, another no-branch bank, racked up the highest customer satisfaction scores of any bank in Canada. Sadly, Loblaw abandoned the partnership in 2018, mainly because CIBC had gradually allowed its advantage to slip away even though the bank captured the largest share of the profits. After the dot-com bubble burst in 2001, CIBC failed to invest in the technology needed to maintain President's Choice Financial's advantage, preferring instead to chase after sexier but also riskier business in the capital markets.

At the heart of the board's choice of Al Flood's successor – and at the heart of CIBC's governance problem – was an irreconcilable conflict of interest. Like many other big Canadian companies, CIBC had a history of cozy relationships with its directors. In the 1970s, the bank found itself in serious trouble as a result of losses on loans to the venerable farm-equipment maker Massey-Ferguson, whose chief executive also happened to be a director of the bank. A few years later, the hit came from Calgary-based Dome Petroleum, another company whose CEO, Jack Gallagher, sat on the bank's board.[9] The bank again came perilously close in the early 1990s to draining all its capital on bad loans to Olympia & York. Same story – the delinquent company's CEO, Paul Reichmann, was a director of CIBC.[10]

Given the directors' age, compensation, and CEO backgrounds, it was hardly surprising that, time and again, they chose short-term stock performance over longer-term sustainability. Worse, many of them also had ties with outside businesses hungry for CIBC loans. The directors were all too aware that a shift of capital away from corporate banking and capital markets might pose a threat to the flow of funds to their business associates. By their decision, the majority of directors showed they had little interest in CIBC's personal and small-business division, even though it clearly represented the better path to solid, sustainable growth.

So, perhaps I should not have been so surprised that, when it came to choosing Al Flood's successor, the board opted for the candidate who would best represent their own business interests. I learned afterwards that it took three tight votes that April afternoon before the scales tipped in John Hunkin's favor. The wholesale business would continue to receive the lion's share of resources, and the directors could go back to their offices secure in the knowledge that CIBC would continue to make loans to large corporations.

One of the Hunkin management team's first moves was to dismantle the governance-oriented corporate center that had formed the hub of the bank since 1994. Sure enough, CIBC proceeded to aggressively pursue business with companies that were growing rapidly but were on shaky foundations. During the dotcom bubble of the late 1990s, it used Amicus to aggressively grow its US market share without worrying much about the new customers' profitability. These strategies cost shareholders billions when the dotcom bubble burst in 2001.

CIBC took big bets on Enron, Worldcom, and Global Crossing, all of which collapsed within the space of a few years. Besides massive write-downs, the once-proud Canadian bank found itself in deep trouble with regulators. It paid a US$80 million fine to the US

Securities and Exchange Commission in 2003 for its role in manipulating Enron's financial statements. Two years later, it was forced to cough up US$2.4 billion to settle a class-action lawsuit brought by a group of pension funds and investment managers, which noted that systematic fraud by Enron and its officers had led to the loss of billions and the collapse of the company.[11] Just a few days after that settlement, on 1 August 2005, John Hunkin announced his retirement at the age of fifty-nine. When the time came to choose his successor, the board swung to the opposite extreme, installing an ultra-conservative caretaker, Gerry McCaughey.

CIBC shares did indeed top John Hunkin's $100 goal in October 2007. But there was little to be proud of. The bank was now the smallest of the Big Five. Less than a year later came the epic meltdown that blew away and crippled some of the best-known names in global banking. CIBC survived, but it spent the next decade licking its wounds, cutting back left, right, and center, making minimal investments in ground-breaking retail banking technology, and shying away from acquisitions.

The future might have been so much brighter had the directors gone in a different direction on that ill-fated day in April 1999.

CHAPTER TWO

A Broken System

My experience at CIBC led me to wonder whether companies have the dynamism to cope with disruptive change, and whether their boards will ever choose long-term sustainability over short-term results. With the invaluable help of Williams Inference Global, a Chicago-based consultancy, my eyes had been opened to the impact that technology, including the mobile Internet, would have on retail banking.

Williams Inference is a one-of-a-kind business. As its website notes, its starting point "is the identification of anomalies: irregularities, surprises and the unusual. Creating insights about change requires confronting the 'new.' The new has no history, thus it has no experts."[1] Williams seeks to identify those early indicators of change that can easily go unnoticed in today's morass of information overload. Its work gave me a powerful new insight into the world of banking. For example, it became clear to me that Microsoft's perceptive founder, Bill Gates, had hit the nail on the head when he noted that "banking is necessary, banks are not."[2]

Given CIBC's choice of a new chief executive, I would never know whether the transformation underway in its retail bank would have succeeded. Instead, I decided to investigate whether other companies had solved the challenges of disruptive change.

The magnitude of the change wrought by new information and communications technology has the power to transform an industry. Similarly, seismic shifts in the regulatory environment or in social and political attitudes can threaten a company's underlying business model. The digital age is turning out to be just such a tsunami of change, so much so that it is turning almost every industry on its head. To take just one example: since 2000, the world of entertainment – spanning music, books, games, newspapers, television, and movies – has been turned upside down. Apple alone has introduced a dozen revolutionary products that have significantly disrupted these businesses, starting with the iPod, and going on to iTunes and the iPad, the latter an entirely new platform for digital newspapers, magazines, books, and videos.[3] The digital revolution is also ripping through financial and professional services (such as accounting and law), health care, and education, among many others whose business model had barely changed in decades, if not centuries.

The forest-products industry was abuzz with dire predictions of the paperless office as early as the 1980s. It was not until the mid-2000s that demand for paper, especially newsprint, actually began to shrink, but few in the Canadian industry were prepared for the shock, even though the sector was the country's biggest earner of foreign exchange. Despite repeated warnings stretching back two and a half decades, Canada's paper mills had done virtually nothing to prepare for this earth-shaking disruption to their business. The result: many mills have closed and almost all have been forced to restructure their debt, their pension plans, and other obligations. The impact on one-industry towns across the country has been devastating.

Much the same applies to newspaper publishing. Online news sites such as *The Huffington Post*, *Buzzfeed*, and *Business Insider* have revolutionized the business. Between 2005 and 2014 American daily papers lost around $30 billion in advertising. Employment at US newspapers sank from 424,900 in 2000 to 173,700 in September 2016. Yet during the same period, the number of jobs in Internet publishing soared from 29,400 to 206,000.[4] Newspaper publishing companies were selling at record prices at the turn of the millennium, even though few people under thirty-five were bothering to read a paper.

Yet within ten years, many of these companies were either up for sale at bargain-basement prices or were being restructured under creditor protection. Few had noticed the dangers that lurked in the exploding popularity of the Internet.

Music-recording companies were another bunch of dinosaurs. They continued to produce CDs despite their increasingly desperate but failed attempts to shut down file-sharing services. By 2017, CD shipments in the United States were less than one-tenth the number in 2000.[5] Although artists have adjusted their business model by putting more emphasis on live concerts and merchandise sales, record companies still churn out CDs even as Apple demonstrates the pull of iTunes at $1.29 a song.

Then there are the banks, which stubbornly continue to process payments through cumbersome and time-consuming central clearing and settlement systems. I sometimes wonder whether they have purposely closed their eyes and ears to M-Pesa, a mobile-phone–based service that enables users to transfer money immediately, and to other digital payment services, such as Alipay, WeChat, PayPal, Apple Pay, Android Pay, and Samsung Pay (to name just a few).

Likewise, it's hard to believe that Canada's banks still stand guard over 6,000 branches, even though more than eight out of every ten customers prefer to bank online or on their smartphones. A recent US Scratch survey suggests that millennials would rather go to the dentist than visit a bank branch.[6]

All these businesses have had one thing in common: they failed to notice the forces of disruption hurtling toward them. They, and countless others, such as Blockbuster, Kodak, Xerox, Kmart, IBM, and Avon Products, did too little too late to avert disaster until they were forced to act by tumbling share prices, fleeing customers and suppliers, or new regulations. As I delved into their missteps, I couldn't help wondering how different some of them might look today if the directors and C-suite executives had given Williams Inference Global a call. Certainly, they should not be surprised at the questions now being raised about their approach to strategic governance.

Corporate Governance Has Failed to Keep Up

As we have just seen, disruptive technological and social change has brought many once-thriving businesses to their knees. Many analysts and pundits foresaw this shake-up as the Internet took off in the mid-1990s. Yet company boards and management were caught flat-footed for two decades or more as they failed to recognize the looming threat and did little or nothing to avert it. They stood by as one venerable business after another went into decline, with devastating effects on shareholders, workers, pensioners, customers, and suppliers. Equally, they failed dismally to adapt to the tremendous opportunities offered by the information age.

As Cisco's former chief executive John Chambers noted on his retirement in 2015, "Since I become CEO (in 1995), 87 per cent of the companies in the Fortune 500 are off the list. What that says is that companies that don't reinvent themselves will be left behind."[7] Indeed, that fate is befalling more and more of them, according to a 2018 report[8] by Innosight, a consultancy founded by Clayton Christensen. Based on almost a century's worth of market data, the study found that corporations included in the S&P 500 index in 1965 remained in the index for an average of thirty-three years. By 1990, the average tenure had narrowed to twenty years. It dropped to eighteen years in 2012, and Innosight forecasts that it will drop to just twelve years by 2027. Deloitte, the global auditing firm and consultancy, made an even more dire prediction in 2018, suggesting that the average S&P 500 lifespan could soon be less than ten years.[9] At the current churn rate, about half of the stocks in the index will be replaced over the next ten years as we enter "a stretch of accelerating change in which lifespans of big companies are getting shorter than ever."[10]

As Arie de Geus, former head of strategy at Royal Dutch Shell and author of *The Living Company*, observed in 1997,[11]

If you look at them in light of their potential, most commercial corporations are dramatic failures – or at best, underachievers. They exist at a primitive stage of evolution; they develop and exploit only a fraction of their potential. For proof, you need only consider their high mortality rate. The average life expectancy of a multinational corporation – Fortune 500 or its equivalent – is between 40 and 50 years. A full one-third of the companies listed in the 1970 Fortune 500, for instance, had vanished by 1983 – acquired, merged or broken into pieces. Human beings have learned to survive, on average for 75 years or more, but there are very few companies that are that old and flourishing.

In 1989, Michael C. Jensen, wrote a seminal article, "Eclipse of the Public Corporation," for the *Harvard Business Review*. He predicted that

> The last share of publicly traded common stock owned by an individual will be sold in the year 2003, if current trends persist. This forecast may be fanciful (short-term trends never persist), but the basic direction is clear. By the turn of the century, the primacy of public stock ownership in the United States may have all but disappeared.[12]

Jensen's prediction turned out to be a little too dire; publicly traded companies have not disappeared. Nonetheless, their numbers have fallen dramatically. From a peak of more than 8,000 in 1996, the number of companies listed on a US stock exchange has shrunk to around 4,100. Much the same has happened in Canada and the United Kingdom.[13] The blame for the decline lies largely with traditional corporate governance practices, which have fallen woefully short in devising long-term strategies to deal with disruptive change and in managing conflicts of interest between directors, managers, and shareholders.

As Jensen predicted, active investors have flourished. They hold large equity or debt positions, sit on boards of directors, monitor and sometimes dismiss management, engage in setting the long-term strategic direction of the companies they invest in, and sometimes manage the companies themselves. The private equity model is built around highly leveraged financial structures, pay-for-performance compensation systems, substantial equity ownership by managers and directors, and contracts with owners and creditors that limit both cross-subsidization among business units and the waste of free cash flow. Private equity firms now own more than 8,000 US companies, almost twice the number of public companies.[14]

Jensen argued that the public corporation model is not suitable for industries marked by slow long-term growth, where internally generated funds outstrip the opportunities for profitable investment, or where downsizing may be the most productive long-term strategy. History shows that when an industry stops growing, the best use of capital is often to give it back to shareholders to invest in a more promising sector. Yet most directors and managers are notoriously reluctant to take such action. Could that by any chance be because it would put them out of a job?

Almost every established enterprise is under pressure today as the Internet, mobile apps, cloud computing, artificial intelligence, blockchain, robots, 3D printers, and social media undermine long-held assumptions about how best to conduct its business. To make matters worse, these changes are sweeping through almost every part of the economy – transportation, accommodation, health care, education, financial and professional services, and many more. Every company should be ditching old practices and investing in new ones, but few are. One has to wonder whether their directors are asking themselves the tough, age-old question posed by management guru Peter Drucker: "If you weren't already in this business, would you enter it today?" And, if the answer is no, whether any are asking the difficult follow-up question: "What are you going to do about it?"[15]

As Michael Jensen sees it, the conventional twentieth-century model of corporate governance – centered on dispersed public ownership, professional managers without substantial equity holdings, and a board of directors dominated by management-appointed outsiders – remains a viable option for rapidly growing companies with profitable investment opportunities that exceed the cash they generate internally. But information-age businesses like Alphabet, Facebook, Alibaba, and Lyft have rejected the traditional governance model. Instead, they have a capital structure that keeps key decisions in the hands of the founders by allowing them to own a special class of equity with more powerful voting rights than out-side shareholders. Given the conflict-of-interest allegations levelled by investors against special-class shareholders in the past, the need for a root-and-branch overhaul of corporate governance could not be clearer.

The Culprits

The word "governance" derives from the Greek "kybernan" (to steer) and "kybernetes" (pilot or helmsman). In other words, governance refers to the way an organization steers itself, and the people responsible for it – namely the directors – are supposedly its leaders. As two prominent members of the Cadbury Royal Commission, which recommended a set of new governance guidelines for the United Kingdom in 1992, noted,

- "If the board is not taking the company purposefully into the future, who is? It is because of boards' failure to create tomorrow's company out of today's that so many famous names in British industry continue to disappear." (Sir John Harvey-Jones)
- "The board's function is to set the company's aims and objectives and to ensure that they are achieved." (Sir Adrian Cadbury)[16]

The job of taking a company "purposefully into the future" should start with the formulation and adoption of a corporate strategy. Yet remarkably little attention has been paid to precisely how boards can or should fulfill this responsibility.[17]

According to one legal expert, "corporate strategy is the foundation on which all corporate policies should stand and is at the heart of the board leadership function."[18] Michael Porter, Harvard's renowned strategy expert, defines corporate strategy as choosing the "business(es) the company is in and how those business(es) should be organized."[19]

It is the owners or their agents, namely the directors, who must decide how to allocate the company's resources. These choices are especially meaningful during periods of disruptive change. Any director worth his or her salt should be paying attention to the outside forces shaping the company's business environment and responding accordingly either by overhauling the underlying business model or by getting out of that business.

Competitive strategy is not the same as corporate strategy. According to Porter, competitive strategy refers to decisions that make a company different from its rivals or lead it to perform similar activities in different ways to achieve a sustainable competitive advantage. The development and execution of competitive strategy – in other words, where to play and how to win – is the responsibility of management. It is the board's role to ratify competitive strategy and monitor its implementation.

A strategy is not a goal or a target. It is "deliberately choosing a different set of activities to deliver unique value." The definition has been refined further by Roger Martin, former dean of the Rotman School of Management at the University of Toronto, and by Monitor Group (which was founded by Michael Porter and his associates, and with which I was associated for thirteen years): *Strategy is an integrated set of choices that uniquely positions the firm in its industry so as to create sustainable advantage and superior value relative to the competition.*[20]

Most corporate boards review and ratify management's competitive strategies once a year. But they do so in a way that doesn't come close to fulfilling their responsibilities as stewards of the company's long-term well-being. The chair typically does not bother to ask broader corporate strategy questions, such as: "Should we even be in this business? Is our current business model the correct one given the outside pressures on the business? How should we be organized?" Likewise, few chief executives have been willing to put those questions to the board, presumably because they are nervous that they will not get the answers they want.

A Blind Spot: Strategic Risk

Corporate directors are also responsible for dealing with strategic risk, defined by Michael Porter as "a function of how poorly a strategy will perform if the wrong scenario occurs."[21] Companies invariably face unpleasant surprises that threaten to undercut and even destroy their business. These potential setbacks may have been building beneath the surface for years, if not decades. The risk of their becoming reality has escalated over the past few decades, given the profound changes in technology, social attitudes, regulation, and the environment. For example, the future of Canada's oil and gas industry is clearly up in the air as climate change and costs drive consumers to switch to electric cars, environmentalists and Indigenous peoples fight the expansion of pipelines, and more people become aware of the cost of capping stranded oil wells.

Such shocks often force a company to change direction, either by ditching a business or altering its business model. What many directors do not realize, however, is that doing nothing is almost always a bigger gamble than embarking on a risky transformation. The earlier they detect these shifts and adjust to them, the more likely the company is to survive. For all companies, according to Mark Zuckerberg, founder and CEO of Facebook, "the biggest risk is not taking any risk ... In a world that is changing really quickly, the only strategy that is guaranteed to fail is not taking risks."[22]

Ever since the Renaissance, scientists have been working to transform the perception of risk from "chance of loss" into "opportunity for gain"; from fate and original design to sophisticated, probability-based forecasts of the future; and from helplessness to choice.[23] Most recently, we have devised sophisticated tools to try to predict the future, among them chaos theory, genetic algorithms, and neural networks. These methods focus largely on the nature of volatility, and their execution stretches the capability of even the most high-powered computers. Even so, these tools, no matter how innovative, have yet to prove very helpful in predicting the impact of disruptive change on human behavior, including business decisions.

According to Michael Jensen, only four forces are able to push back against management decisions that fail to recognize long-term shareholder and societal interests:

- capital markets;
- legal, political, or regulatory action;

- customers, suppliers, and employees; and
- internal controls put in place by the board of directors.[24]

Some of these are more effective than others. The ability of capital markets to influence business decisions is constrained by law and regulatory practice. The legal, political, and regulatory system is far too blunt an instrument to deal with wasteful or self-interested corporate behavior. Customers, suppliers, and employees may be slow to exercise discipline on a wayward business, but their influence is ultimately inescapable. Firms that do not supply the product that customers desire at a competitive price cannot survive. The trouble is, by the time market forces take effect, it is often too late to save the enterprise.

That leaves the board's internal controls to do the job. There is substantial evidence that the normal control systems in public corporations have generally failed to keep managers on the track of long-term survival and growth. Few firms have ever transformed themselves or shifted direction without being forced to do so by a crisis in the environment around them.[25]

If there is a key to successful risk taking, it is that those who expose a business to risk or respond to risk always have a single purpose in mind – to enhance the long-term value of the business. If the decision makers are not aligned with the interests of the owners, the business will invariably suffer. It will be exposed to some risks that it should have avoided and not exposed to others that it should have exploited. Knowing which way to go can be a difficult job, especially in large, complex public (and private) companies. The interests of top management may not be the same as those of colleagues lower down the ladder, and both may have priorities that differ markedly from those of shareholders and creditors. Ultimately, it is up to the board of directors to manage those competing interests.

Green Shoots of Renewal

In 1994, the Toronto Stock Exchange asked Peter Dey, a prominent lawyer and former chair of the Ontario Securities Commission, to produce guidelines for improved corporate governance in Canada.[26]

His fourteen recommendations became required practice for all companies listed on the TSX. Most important, every board was required to issue an annual statement of corporate governance practices disclosing the extent to which it had followed the guidelines. The exchange and the Institute of Corporate Directors followed up in 1999 with a study that reviewed governance practices among TSX-listed companies. Sadly, it concluded that many fell short of the 1995 guidelines and, as a result, the exchange issued a more explicit directive in 2002 (updated in 2009). It read in part,

> The board of directors of every corporation should explicitly assume responsibility for the stewardship of the corporation and as part of the overall stewardship responsibility, should assume responsibility for the following matters:
>
> (i)   Adoption of a corporate strategy;
> (ii) Succession planning, including appointing, training and monitoring senior management;
> (iii) A communications program for the corporation;
> (iv) The integrity of the corporation's internal control and management information systems.[27]

However, amendments to the Canada Business Corporations Act (CBCA) in 2005, aimed at codifying a national standard for corporate governance, watered down the TSX guidelines. The board, the CBCA stipulated, was responsible only for "adopting a strategic planning process and approving a strategic plan ... which takes into account ... the opportunities and risks of the business."[28] In other words, boards had only to put a strategic-planning process in place; they were not held responsible for the overall stewardship and sustainability of the corporation. Yet most strategic-planning processes assume that the business is a going concern, without considering possible disruptive forces at play.

There is a debate in some countries whether directors have a duty beyond providing short-term value for shareholders.[29] Canada's Supreme Court has made it clear that they have no such obligation. It ruled in 2008 that a group of Bell Canada bondholders had no recourse against the company after a proposed leveraged buyout diminished the value of their investments. The UK Companies Act requires company directors to promote the success of the business for the benefit of its members – in other words, shareholders. But in doing so, they must take six specific factors into account: the long-term consequences of their decisions; the interests of employees; relationships with customers and suppliers; the impact of corporate activities on the community and environment; the company's reputation for high standards of business conduct; and the need for fair treatment of all stakeholders.[30]

Most boards accept that the development and execution of business unit strategy – in other words, where the existing business plays and how it wins – is management's responsibility. The board's role is to ratify (with appropriate due diligence) and monitor the implementation of that competitive strategy. More problematic is the question who bears responsibility for corporate strategy – that is, for assessing whether a company is in the wrong business (or in the right business, but doing it the wrong way), and for taking timely action.

Boards, especially in the United States, have come to recognize the need to manage strategic risk, but most still fall far short. A recent survey by PricewaterhouseCoopers of 860 boards of public companies found that strategic planning topped directors' wish list for better ways to do their job. More than three-quarters of respondents wanted to spend more time on planning in the coming year.[31] According to a McKinsey global survey of directors in 2011, 44 per cent of respondents said that their involvement in formulating strategy went no further than reviewing and approving management's proposals. But seven in ten said they wanted to spend more time on strategy, making it their primary area of focus. A follow-up survey in 2013 confirmed that most directors are not meeting their most basic responsibility:

A mere 34% of the 772 directors surveyed … agreed that the boards on which they served fully comprehended their companies' strategies. Only 22% said their boards were completely aware of how their firms created value, and just 16% claimed that their boards had a strong understanding of the dynamics of their firms' industries.[32]

McKinsey's 2018 survey of 1,100 directors found that board practices have changed little.[33] This is a terrible indictment. Understanding the company's strategy is among the most basic requirements for directors to fulfill their fiduciary duty to shareholders. Most legal codes stress two core aspects of duty: loyalty (placing the company's interests ahead of one's own) and prudence (applying proper care, skill, and diligence to business decisions). "Nothing suggests that the role of a loyal and prudent director is to pressure management to maximize short-term shareholder value to the exclusion of any other interest. To the contrary, the logical implication is that he or she should help the company thrive for years into the future."[34]

Lessons from the Frog

Many analysts and pundits foresaw the disruptive changes wrought by the information age, but the same cannot be said for business leaders. As the German theoretical physicist Max Planck plaintively remarked, "A new scientific truth does not triumph by convincing its opponents and making them see the light, but rather because its opponents eventually die, and a new generation grows up that is familiar with it."[35]

As American physicist, historian, and philosopher Thomas Kuhn elaborated, "When paradigms change, the world itself changes with them. Led by a new paradigm, scientists adopt new instruments and look in new places. Even more important, during revolutions scientists see new and different things when looking with familiar instruments in places they have looked before."[36] Dialogue plays a special role in shifting paradigms and solving problems that require more shared understanding with others than in the past.[37]

Change often comes slowly, as Warren Buffett intimated when he commented that he did not know who was going to be making money in the auto business in ten years, but he did know who would be number one in soft drinks and number one in chewing gum.[38] Buffett's point was that while the war against obesity may have an impact on soft-drink sales, whatever changes result will take place over many years. Sometimes change happens fast, as it did with smartphones. The business model shifted from hardware to software almost overnight with the introduction of the iPhone 3G.

The toughest challenge in the business world is for corporate directors dealing with an industry that is changing at a rate somewhere between fast (smartphones) and slow (chewing gum). Between the challenge of predicting the future and the deceptively slow pace at which disruptive change often occurs, the oft-told story of the boiled frog seems apposite. Put the frog in boiling water and it jumps out. Put it in cold water that is slowly brought to a boil and it stays put. The frog does not want to die; it just does not notice the temperature rising until it is too late.*

The frog's behavior helps explain why managers and boards have difficulty dealing with unsettling change. Some put the blame on capitalist greed. As Charles O. Prince, Citigroup's former CEO, infamously put it in July 2007 shortly before the global financial crisis hit: "When the music stops ... things will be complicated. But as long as the music is playing, you've got to get up and dance. We're still dancing."[39] Financial markets and management incentive plans pressure directors and managers to chase short-term earnings growth, but only for as long as the music is playing. When the music stops, things are sure to get messy. But – and here's the rub – no one knows when that will happen.

The fact is that few executives or directors fully appreciate the forces beyond the corporate bubble they inhabit. One of the rare exceptions was A.G. Lafley, former chair and chief executive of Proctor & Gamble, the consumer products giant, who made this perceptive observation: "The CEO is the chief external officer with primary responsibility for translating the meaningful outside into winning strategies for the business and the organization. This means choosing what business or businesses to be in and which to exit, to shut

---

* Although this story has been disproven (https://www.theatlantic.com/technology/archive/2006/09/the-boiled-frog-myth-stop-the-lying-now/7446/), it resonates with observed human behavior.

down, or not to enter." Lafley went on to note that "in contrast to the CEO, most company employees are inward-focused. The content of their work and the nature of their working relationships inevitably draw their attention inside the company."[40]

Jack Welch, legendary chair and CEO of General Electric (GE) from 1980 to 2001, was a master in showing how the board and senior management could work together to move a company forward. Welch and his colleagues in GE's corporate center would review each business segment to determine if it had a competitive strategy that would make it number one or number two in its industry. If not, the business was sold, closed, or fixed. The board's job, with the help of the corporate center, was to allocate resources, primarily capital and people, to those businesses best placed to create value for shareholders. The performance of GE's stock showed just how successful Welch was in doing that, soaring forty-fold during his twenty-one-year tenure.

Welch's successor, Jeff Immelt, was less fortunate, noting in a 2015 interview,

> The world is so doggone different today than it was 10, 15 or 20 years ago. I would say no matter what you are running, you control fewer things. And so, you need to be more resilient. Jack was a great CEO, but he really controlled his world. It was a centralized kind of command-and-control company. Those days are over. I'm in the risk management business. Governments are more active. The world is more difficult. You are not in the control business today, you're in the risk-reward business.[41]

Immelt undoubtedly spoke the truth, but he struggled to live up to it. During his tenure, GE stock lost half its value.

Activists Take Up the Slack

Immelt did everything by the book to adapt to the changing environment, including embracing internal start-ups to foster innovation. Yet investors had gotten tired of waiting for results. Instead, they poured billions into disruptive – yet loss-making – newcomers such as Amazon, Uber, and Tesla. Perhaps, as Edgar Schein, the expert on organizational culture at MIT's Sloan School of Management, said decades ago, it is almost impossible to change corporate culture and transform a company without changing all of its people.[42] After sixteen years of GE's trying to transform itself, the company's time was up. In 2017, an activist hedge fund, Trian Partners, bought 1.5 per cent of the venerable company's stock, enough to give it significant influence over such a widely held company.

My colleague David Beatty, chair of the David and Sharon Johnston Centre for Corporate Governance Innovation at the Rotman School of Management in Toronto, links the rise of insurgent investors like Trian Partners directly to the failure of directors to do their job:

> Boards of directors have always represented the shareholders in publicly-traded companies, validating financial results, protecting their assets, and counseling the CEO. It's a tough and demanding responsibility, requiring individual directors to learn as much as they can about a company and its operations so that their insights and advice can stand up alongside those of executives. That, at least, is the ideal.
>
> One litmus test of whether or not the ideal is coming anywhere close to being the reality is the growth and involvement of "activist investors." Simply put, if boards were doing their jobs, there would be no activist opportunities. However, they are apparently doing badly enough that there has been huge growth in activist firms.[43]

Activist directors – a separate breed from activist investors – have real work to do. They must decide how to allocate the firm's scarce resources, notably capital and executive talent.

I have worked on corporate strategy with half a dozen activist directors in different industries over the past twenty years. Because they represented sizable minority shareholders, they were able to force their fellow directors to put the company's corporate strategy on the board agenda. Whenever they did so, the board would consider several options, including management's option (typically a version of the status quo), a sale, and something in between. In my experience, when directors come to understand the outside forces at play in their company's future, and then evaluate different options, they are usually quite willing to make the necessary tough decisions, including selling the company or a large chunk of it.

But as my research on the residential mortgage industry showed, directors cannot rely on managers to detect disruptive change nor to prepare the organization for transformation. The next two chapters explain why managers' inherent conflicts of interest make it difficult for them to discern changes in the environment, or to act on them. For that reason, it is hard to imagine many CEOs advising their board to harvest, exit, or transform a key business. That leaves only the board to make such difficult decisions, no matter what internal controls may be in place to nudge management in the right direction.

As Dominic Barton, McKinsey's former global managing partner, has said,

> If only directors could keep their fiduciary duty to shareholders firmly in mind, big changes in the boardroom would surely follow. They would spend more time discussing disruptive innovations in the world beyond that could lead to new goods, services, markets and business models. They would grill both themselves and senior management on what it would take to capture opportunities with a big upside over the long term and, conversely, which operations no longer fit. And they would spend less time talking about peripheral issues like how to meet next quarter's earnings expectations, or how to comply with regulations, or how to avoid lawsuits.[44]

Choices, Choices ...

Applying Joseph Schumpeter's theory of creative destruction, directors have just three choices when disruptive change threatens to up-end their company. The first is to head for the exits early on, selling the business before the disruption becomes obvious to all. Alternatively, the company can continue to harvest as much profit as possible until the disruption becomes obvious to all and activist investors move in to break up the business, separating the wheat from the chaff. The final option is for the board to push the company in a new direction so that it becomes a leader rather than a laggard, and its own "creative destroyer." History has shown the difficulty of transforming an industrial-age company into an information-age one, but, as we shall see in later chapters, I believe it can be done using a fresh approach to governance.

Regrettably, the easiest and usually most travelled route is to carry on doing what worked in the past. This choice invariably leads to steady decline – think Kodak, Blockbuster, Kmart, Xerox, Sears, and, in Canada, Blackberry, Abitibi-Price, Eaton's, and many others. The industry may survive, but no matter how hard it tries to preserve the status quo, it will keep going downhill until it is a mere shadow of its former self.

CHAPTER THREE

When Seeing Is Not Believing

Turbulent times are nothing new. Heraclites (535–475 BCE), a pre-Socratic Ionian philosopher known for his observation that change is central to the universe, noted that the world is in a continual state of flux. He illustrated his point with a metaphor: "One cannot step in the same river twice."

Some might argue that social upheaval has intensified with the advent of scientific thinking, the onset of the Industrial Revolution in the eighteenth century, and, most recently, the advance of information and communications technology. In fact, new technologies and profound social change have buffeted humankind since time immemorial. But there is no doubt that the disruptions have become more severe as economic and social upheavals are exacerbated by other fundamental challenges: climate change, ozone depletion, ocean acidification, and species extinction, not to mention dramatic scientific and technological breakthroughs. All in all, we face a far more complex and uncertain environment than even our grandparents did.

In a corporate context, dealing with this uncertainty and the risks it creates is one of the primary responsibilities of the board of directors. They must be on the lookout for signs that these shifts are occurring, and then make sure that management responds before it is too late. Before that can happen however, directors need to understand what disruptive change is and how it takes place so that they recognize it when they see it.

What Is Disruptive Change?

Disruptive change refers to any process that undermines the fundamental properties or states of a system. It might include, among others, new technology, regulation, legislation, and fast-evolving social and political attitudes, any of which has the potential to threaten the underlying business model of a company, or even an entire industry.

Keeping track of disruptive change is especially critical in this day and age because all these forces are moving faster and more dramatically than ever before. The McKinsey Global Institute argues that four fundamental forces – accelerating technological change, urbanization, an aging population, and globalization – are changing the world more rapidly and profoundly than most people can grasp.[1] McKinsey estimates that change in the modern era is happening ten times faster than during the Industrial Revolution and at three hundred times the scale, giving it roughly three thousand times the impact. Much as waves can amplify one another, these trends are growing in strength, magnitude, and influence as they crash against one another. Together they are unleashing forces that have a profound impact on almost every business on earth.

If directors are to determine the appropriate response to disruption, they should ideally understand how disruptive change takes place. Harvard's Clayton Christensen, one of the foremost experts in the field, singles out disruptive innovation to explain how new entrants use technology to overtake incumbents. On another front, the theory of creative destruction described by Joseph Schumpeter, the Austrian economist and political scientist, shows how entrepreneurs and innovators disrupt established industries. Far-reaching innovations, known as general-purpose technologies, can totally destroy existing industries and spawn the growth of entirely new ones. These changes, which can take place simultaneously, create the turbulent environment that business faces today and the strategic risk that directors should be concerned about. To illustrate each of these theories, I will use examples from the financial-services industry also described in my earlier book *Stumbling Giants*.

Disruptive Innovation

Clayton Christensen has argued that firms which generate profits from established technologies are at a disadvantage against aggressive upstarts with fresh ideas. Christensen singles out two types of disruption – "low-end disruption" targeted at customers who have no need for services valued by high-end customers and are unwilling to pay for them; and "new-market disruption" aimed at customers not served by existing businesses.

Recent developments in the financial-payments system illustrate both "low-end" and "new-market" disruptive technology. Over the past decade, eight out of every ten adults in Kenya have come to use M-Pesa, a form of mobile money that is sent from cellphone to cellphone using a simple text-messaging system.[2] M-Pesa has become so popular that some experts estimate it handles almost half of Kenya's GDP. Similar systems have sprouted up across Africa and Asia, particularly in countries where regular financial markets are close to collapse, such as Zimbabwe and Somalia.

Transactions on M-Pesa typically involve only small amounts of money, but nimble start-ups have noticed that servicing millions of people, even poor ones, can be quite lucrative. About 2.5 billion adults around the world, or more than half of earth's adult population, do not have a bank account. The popularity of mobile phones, combined with advances in cloud-computing and data-crunching technology, have dramatically lowered the cost of lending to these people, as well as of transferring and storing their money. These services do not bring the unbanked into the financial mainstream so much as they broaden the mainstream to embrace the unbanked – an example of new-market disruption.

Mobile payments are wooing not only "low-end" and "unbanked" consumers. In Asia, payment apps are a way of life for more than a billion users. In the West, mobile banking is reaching critical mass – 49 per cent of Americans already use their phones for banking transactions – and tech giants are muscling in. Apple unveiled a credit card with Goldman Sachs in March 2019. Facebook has proposed a payments service to let users buy tickets and settle bills.

Similarly, Apple, Android, and Samsung have introduced payment applications for smartphones over the past few years. These apps store payment-card credentials and use wireless technology to generate payments. Users need only be near a suitable terminal to initiate a transaction, then enter a PIN, pattern, or password for authentication, or just a fingerprint or retina scan on devices with a sensor. This approach to payments is not only faster and safer than traditional debit- and credit-card transactions but also more secure, thus overcoming the biggest concerns of traditional bank customers.

According to Christensen, small competitors that nibble away at the periphery of an industry can normally be ignored, with one crucial caveat. If they are on a disruptive trajectory, they pose a mortal threat to incumbents.[3] Because innovation is a process, with the new product or service evolving over time, forward-thinking incumbents can be quite creative in defending their franchise. Disrupters tend to focus on creating the right business model, rather than just the right product. When they succeed, they move from the fringe (the low end of the market or a new market) to the mainstream, first eroding incumbents' market share and then their profitability. This process can take years, usually giving incumbent directors and managers plenty of time to devise an effective response. Christensen cautions corporate leaders to beware of overreacting to disruption by dismantling a still-profitable business. Instead they should strengthen relationships with their core customers and set up a new business unit to take advantage of growth opportunities spawned by the disruption.[4]

According to *The Economist*, the benefits of technological change in financial services will be vast, and are rapidly making themselves felt. Costs are likely to tumble as branches are shut, creaking mainframe systems retired, and bureaucracies culled. If the biggest banks are able to chop expenses by a third, every person on earth will save US$80 a year.[5] Given the magnitude of the opportunity, new entrants are lining up.

Creative Destruction

Schumpeter described creative destruction as "the process of industrial mutation that incessantly revolutionizes the economic structure from within, incessantly destroying the old one, incessantly creating a new one."[6] The process starts with spurts in entrepreneurial behavior that disrupt established industries. The upheavals completely transform the affected industry, culminating in the emergence of a new set of more efficient, customer-friendly players.[7] Indeed, history is littered with waves of innovation that have reinvigorated tired industries, boosted productivity, and spurred economic growth.[8] But experience suggests that very few incumbents have been able to make the transition. As a result, most fall by the wayside.

Creative destruction helps to explain a key dynamic in the business world – namely, the transition from a competitive to a monopolistic or oligopolistic market, and back again. Healthy economies and industries go through cycles where destruction of the old order releases a burst of creativity. After a phase of growth, followed by a period of consolidation, pressure typically builds from customers and suppliers for far-reaching change. Resistance to that change inevitably leads to what C.S. Holling, a founder of ecological economics, called a "rigidity trap," putting the company or industry into a death spiral.[9]

Most of us are inclined to view a forest fire, a General Motors plant closure, or a bank failure as an unmitigated disaster with few, if any, silver linings. But while such setbacks may destroy some powerful structures, they also release trapped resources – whether nutrients or ideas or money – that spawn new life. For example, while mainstream banks were preoccupied with meeting the stricter capital and liquidity ratios imposed after the 2008 financial crisis, thousands of fintech entrepreneurs, many of them backed by deep-pocketed venture-capital funds and other investors, were busily building new lending, investing, and payments mechanisms. This burst of innovation now threatens to leave the banks even farther behind.

General-Purpose Technologies

The Canadian Institute for Advanced Research has coined the term "general-purpose technologies," often abbreviated to GPTs, to describe earth-shaking innovations with the potential to transform business across a wide range of sectors.[10] Examples include the printing press, electricity, railways, the internal combustion engine, and, most recently, the computer, the Internet, and neural networks. GPTs are not confined to technologies that we can touch or see. They may also apply to ways of thinking about and applying knowledge.

GPTs have four essential attributes: the scope to make vast improvements, a wide variety of uses, applications across a broad cross-section of the economy, and the ability to feed off and influence other technologies. Further research has validated the link between GPTs and Schumpeter's theory of creative destruction.[11]

One important consequence of technological progress is the accelerating obsolescence of capital – whether in the form of property, machines and equipment, or human knowledge.[12] To make matters worse, powerful oligopolies can use their clout to resist adoption of disruptive new technologies, not only putting a brake on productivity but also pushing their industry into a "rigidity trap." As I have repeatedly suggested in earlier chapters and in my other books, the Canadian banks are a prime example of such resistance.

Since both obsolescence and progress are central to Schumpeter's concept of creative destruction, they have a big impact on how long it takes to adopt a new general-purpose technology and the costs of doing so. The normal period for new technologies to be understood, adopted, and integrated into production is twenty to thirty years, as was the case with the personal computer and, most recently, the Internet.[13] More recent GPTs, such as the mobile Internet and cloud computing, suggest that pace of adoption is accelerating.

Though these cycles may seem obvious to many of us, corporate directors and managers often profess to be shocked by changes in the external environment. In one sense, that is not surprising given the glacial pace at which complex systems adjust to GPTs and other disruptive forces. Could it be that managers and boards, like the frog in hot water, do in fact notice the changes unfolding around them but cannot comprehend or deal with the consequences for their businesses, and thus end up doing nothing until it is too late?

Take the 2008 financial crisis. Even the top US policy makers – former Federal Reserve chairman Alan Greenspan and treasury secretaries Robert Rubin and Timothy Geithner – have acknowledged that they failed to see the consequences of the burgeoning shadow banking system until the global financial crisis had struck. The fragmentation of the home mortgage sector from a vertically integrated business conducted by regulated banks into half a dozen separate components left large parts of the sector unregulated. The emergence of mortgage-backed securities and the nimble – but all too often unscrupulous – firms that issued them put the global financial system into a tailspin once US house prices started to tumble in 2007. It's hard to believe that so many supposed experts could have been so badly blindsided, especially when almost three-quarters of residential mortgages were in the hands of the unregulated shadow banking sector.

As far back as the 1970s, traditional banking – in other words, taking deposits and making loans – began to be overshadowed by the bundling of assets, which could be sold to investors as securities in a process known as securitization. This concept paved the way for whiz kids on Wall Street to create entirely new classes of financial instruments: mortgage and other asset-backed securities; high-yield or junk bonds that drove leveraged buyouts and the private equity boom; and derivative instruments, such as interest rate, currency, credit, and liquidity swaps that changed the way risks were managed. The foundations for this transformation were laid in the 1970s by two earth-shaking innovations – modern portfolio theory and computing technology – which triggered massive growth in the financial-services industry.

Supercharged by advances in computing and communications technology and by falling international trade barriers, securitization fueled the globalization of capital markets. As the world economy became more integrated, new technology and access to new markets propelled cross-border capital flows. Between 1990 and 2007, global financial assets almost quadrupled from US$56 trillion to US$206 trillion, a growth rate of roughly 8 per cent a year. The 2008 meltdown brought that pell-mell growth to an abrupt halt, but the financial markets have subsequently resumed their growth, with asset values regaining their 2007 level in 2018.[14]

As the financial meltdown showed, when managers, directors, and regulators are confronted with a forest, they all too often see only the trees, failing to grasp that they are part of something much bigger. But noticing the forest is essential if these supposed stewards of good governance are to respond before it is too late.

Artificial Intelligence Is Next

A new wave of general-purpose technologies, in the form of artificial intelligence (AI), is rapidly making itself felt. It has the potential to change the world at an exponential pace,[15] at a time when we do not yet have an effective corporate governance model for earlier GPTs. Imagine the mess if organizations attempt to navigate the next wave of change without the ability to steer. Our current means of governance and its supporting regulatory structures are not designed to cope with disruption on this scale.[16]

Deep learning based on neural networks and other AI architectures are being applied to a widening variety of human endeavors, where they have produced results comparable to and in some cases superior to human experts.

Ajay Agrawal, an entrepreneurship expert at the University of Toronto's Rotman School of Management, takes the view that AI serves a single, but potentially transformative, purpose: namely, it significantly lowers the cost of prediction. He compares its impact with that of semiconductors, noting that both have dramatically lowered the cost of a useful input and, as a result, ushered in far-reaching changes right across society.[17]

Semiconductors reduced the cost of arithmetic, causing three things to happen. First, applications that already used arithmetic could now handle much, much more, vastly expanding their power and efficiency. These applications were originally used for government and military purposes – for example, putting a man on the moon. Later, they could be used for more mundane functions such as demand forecasting and cashflow projections.

Second, we started using this cheaper arithmetic to solve problems that had not previously been framed as arithmetical problems. For example, chemicals once formed the basis of film-based photography. Then, as arithmetic became cheaper, we began using arithmetic-based solutions to design digital cameras, with devastating effect on companies like Kodak, which hadn't seen them coming.

The plummeting cost of arithmetic has also changed the relative value of other items by boosting the worth of complementary technologies but diminishing the value of substitutes. In the case of photography, the complements were the software and hardware used in digital cameras. These rose in value because we used more of them, while the value of substitutes, the chemical components of film-based cameras, went down as we had less and less use for them.

As the cost of prediction continues to drop, we will use even more AI in a wide range of applications such as investment management and supply chains because it enables us to calculate future scenarios faster, more reliably, and at lower cost. At the same time, we'll start using predictive tools to solve problems that have not, until now, been considered suitable for this kind of treatment. For example, we never thought of autonomous driving as a prediction problem (if we thought of it at all). But AI needs to predict the answer to only one question: "What would a good human driver do?" An AI system makes a lot of mistakes at first. But it learns from its mistakes and updates its model every time it incorrectly predicts the action that a human would have taken. Its predictions get better and better until it becomes so good at predicting what a human would do that we no longer need a human to do the job. AI can eventually perform the action all by itself, with no loss of accuracy or safety.

The implications for society are huge. The full impact of AI on business, jobs, education, health care, and even democracy has yet to become apparent. But one thing is clear: to be relevant in the AI era, most companies will have to transform themselves. And as I show in this book, corporate transformations to date are rare.

Without more effective governance, not only will existing companies fail, but new companies will find it challenging to keep up with the exponential pace of change.

Failure to Detect Disruptive Change

According to American physicist, historian, and philosopher Thomas Kuhn, "discovery commences with the awareness of anomaly."[18] Kuhn's point was that science seldom progresses in a linear and continuous way but periodically undergoes unexpected "paradigm shifts" that open up new approaches to understanding. Our comprehension of science, so Kuhn's argument goes, can never rely on "objectivity" alone but must also take account of subjective perspectives based on the different world views of researchers and participants.

Or to put it another way, we often "see" things only when and where we want to find them. Consider Edgar Allan Poe's story *The Purloined Letter*. Desperate searchers were certain that the letter in question must have been squirrelled away in a secret hiding place: under the wallpaper, in the floorboards, or inside a piece of furniture. Yet it was hiding in plain sight in a letter box near the suspect's writing table. The searchers' preconceived notions of reality did not allow for such an outcome, so they never saw it. Applying Thomas Kuhn's theory, Poe's "purloined letter" was an anomaly; it didn't conform to the searchers' expectations. Likewise, corporate managers and directors are all too often conditioned to look for information that supports their worldview or prejudices rather than for data that might upset their strategies.

In his book *Emotional Intelligence*, Daniel Coleman notes how often we act before we think. Neuroscientists have isolated a part of the brain, the amygdala, as a gatekeeper that previews data before they are passed to the neo-cortex, the thinking corner of the brain. This can be a lifesaver if we're confronting a lunging tiger or some other imminent danger. When, however, we encounter the unusual – say, a red five of spades[19] or a dog that didn't bark during a crime[20] – the amygdala all too often tends to block our perception of reality. Our discomfort with the unfamiliar creates a natural avoidance mechanism. For much the same reason, I believe, bankers and regulators failed to pay attention to the disruption of the residential mortgage industry until 2007, when the financial system had already begun its meltdown.

The Nobel laureate Daniel Kahneman has pointed out that human decisions are usually made based on limited, often unreliable information and are further hampered by internal limits (the brain's processing power) and external limits (for example, time constraints). As a result, we have developed a subconscious strategy, a problem-solving aid for just such situations: we rely on cognitive shortcuts known as heuristics.

Heuristics are rules of thumb that allow us to simplify the decision-making process. For example, the availability heuristic – how available are examples for comparison – and our ease of access to this information form a significant portion of our foundation for assessment. Confirmation bias, the tendency to search for or interpret information in a way that confirms our preconceptions, is a common example. Then there is anchoring: the predilection for relying too heavily on one piece of information when making decisions. Clearly these biases get in the way of identifying disruptive change even when it should be obvious.

As Kuhn points out, anomalies can only be identified after they have happened. Even so, history can open the mind to future possibilities. As the prominent German philosopher Gottfried Leibniz cautioned in 1703, "Nature has established patterns originating in the return of events, but only for the most part."[21] The caveat is critical, for without it there would be no risk because everything would be predictable. Without it, there would be no change, because every event would be identical to a previous event. The effort to comprehend nature's tendency to repeat itself, but only imperfectly, is what "seeing" is all about. A deep understanding of history, including its anomalies and imperfections, would help directors and managers understand what might happen in the future, giving them time to react before their comfortable world slides from underneath them.

Let's return to the 2008 financial crisis to illustrate the power of history. In their 1991 book, *Generations: The History of America's*

Future, American historians William Strauss and Neil Howe sought to locate patterns that recur over time and to discover the natural rhythms of social experience. They observed that modern history has followed a remarkable pattern, in which, over the past five centuries, Anglo-American society entered a new era – a new turning – every two decades or so. At the start of each turning, people changed how they felt about themselves, the culture, the nation, and the future. According to Strauss and Howe, turnings come in cycles of four. Each cycle spans the length of a long human life, roughly eighty to one hundred years, a unit of time the ancients called the saeculum. Together, the four turnings of the saeculum compose history's seasonal rhythm of growth, maturation, entropy, and destruction.[22]

Building on this historical pattern, Strauss and Howe made the following prediction in 1995:

Sometime around the year 2005, perhaps a few years before or after, America will enter the Fourth Turning ... A spark will ignite a new mood. Today (1995), the same spark would flame briefly but then extinguish, its last flicker merely confirming and deepening the unraveling-era mindset. This time, though, it will catalyze a Crisis. In retrospect, the spark might seem as ominous as a financial crash, as ordinary as a national election, or as trivial as a Tea Party.

This implosion will strike financial markets – and, with that, the economy. Aggressive individualism, institutional decay, and long-term pessimism can proceed only so far before a society loses the level of dependability needed to sustain the division of labor and long-term promises on which a market economy must rest. Through the Unraveling, people will have preferred (or, at least, tolerated) the exciting if bewildering trend toward social complexity. But as the Crisis mood congeals, people will come to the jarring realization that they have grown helplessly dependent on a teetering edifice of anonymous transactions and paper guarantees. Many Americans won't know where their savings are, who their employer is, what their pension is, or how their government works. The era will have left the financial world arbitraged and tentacled: Debtors won't know who holds their notes; homeowners who owns their mortgages and shareholders who runs their equities – and vice versa.[23]

This prophecy was made more than a decade before the subprime mortgage crisis, yet it describes perfectly the situation in September 2008. The lesson is that by using history to shine a light on the future, the perceptive among us can indeed recognize anomalies that foreshadow future upheavals.

Companies are history-dependent complex ecosystems connected to a myriad of stakeholders. They are shaped and influenced by where they have been.[24] For example, an organization's culture is largely embedded by its founders, and it is reluctant to change even when the external environment changes dramatically. But much of traditional management theory ignores this point, instead suggesting that directors and managers lead cultural change using traditional process re-engineering. Schumpeter reinforces this point in the following quotation:

> The usual theorist's paper and the usual government commission's report never try to see that behavior – on the one hand, as a result of a piece of past history and, on the other hand, as an attempt to deal with a situation that is sure to change presently – is an attempt by those firms to keep on their feet, on ground that is slipping away from under them. In other words, the problem that is usually being visualized is how capitalism administers existing structures, whereas the relevant problem is how it creates and destroys them. As long as this is not recognized, the investigator does a meaningless job. As soon as it is recognized, his outlook on capitalist practice and its social results changes considerably.[25]

Prior to 2008, bankers and regulators constructed their business strategies and future projections on the assumption that the well-worn model of the vertically integrated residential-mortgage business would continue for many years to come. They did not even consider, much less foresee, that the old model might fragment and give way to a whole new world. As one academic succinctly observed, "Environments often surprise organizations."[26]

Our ingrained ideas of reality limit and shape our perceptions of the world and ourselves.[27] These constraints manifest themselves in two ways. In some cases, we are totally blind to reality; in others, we see reality but fail to act on it. Karl Weick, a professor of organizational behavior at the University of Michigan, puts it another way: "The realization obviously is affected by the quality of the ideas one carries to the microcosm and 'sees' in its unfolding (believing is seeing)."[28]

Applying these theories to the practicalities of the business world implies that managers depend on two hard-wired processes for decision making.[29] First, the brain uses *pattern recognition*, a complex process that integrates information from as many as thirty different parts of the brain to make assumptions based on prior experiences. Those assumptions tend to determine how people respond to any given situation. The second process, known as *emotional tagging*, determines which emotions attach themselves to the thoughts and experiences stored in our memories. "This emotional information tells us whether to pay attention to something or not, and it tells us what sort of action we should be contemplating (immediate or postponed, fight or flight)."[30] Much of this process is subconscious, making it hard to check the data and logic we use as we go through the process of making a decision.

Neuroscience research has also demonstrated that a full 80 to 90 per cent of what we think we see is generated by patterns already embedded in the brain rather than what our eyes actually see. A famous Harvard University experiment proved the point several years ago. Participants were asked to watch a short video in which six people – three in white shirts and three in black shirts – toss basketballs around. They were told to keep a silent count of the number of passes made by the people in white shirts. At some point, a gorilla ambles into the middle of the action, faces the camera, thumps its chest, and then leaves, spending nine seconds on screen. Afterwards, participants were asked if they saw the gorilla. Fully half of them counted the passes but had no recollection of seeing the animal. It was as though the gorilla were invisible.[31]

As neuroscientists often put it, we do not always see what our eyes see; we see what our *brain* sees. This phenomenon has been summarized by Atul Gawande, an American brain surgeon, writer, and public-health researcher:[32]

> If visual sensations were primarily received rather than constructed by the brain, you'd expect that most of the fibres going to the brain's primary visual cortex would come from the retina. Instead, scientists have found that only twenty per cent do; eighty per cent come downward from regions of the brain governing functions like memory. Richard Gregory, a prominent British neuropsychologist, estimates that visual perception is more than ninety per cent memory and less than ten per cent sensory nerve signals.

What the brain supplies to our perception of the world comes from what neuroscientists term "invariant representations" – the models the brain uses to create our perceptions. Jeff Hawkins, founder of the Redwood Center for Theoretical Neuroscience and of Palm Computing, illustrates this point by explaining what happens when a baseball player catches a ball:

> When a ball is thrown, three things happen. First, the appropriate memory is automatically recalled by the sight of the ball. Second, the memory actually recalls a temporal sequence of muscle commands. And third, the retrieved memory is adjusted as it is recalled to accommodate the particulars of the moment, such as the ball's actual path and the position of your body. The memory of how to catch a ball was not programmed into your brain, it was learned over years of repetitive practice, and it is stored, not calculated, in your neurons.[33]

In summary, the mental models the brain uses to make predictions are constrained and shaped by our worldview and frames of reference – in other words, by our network of ideas, beliefs, social and cultural prejudices, and taken-for-granted assumptions about the world around us. As Hawkins says; "Everything you know and have learned is stored in this model."[34]

Before we can even consider acting, we must first understand the need for a different perspective. Although it is usually impossible to predict specific events, such as the US subprime-mortgage crisis, it is certainly possible to detect anomalies and recognize patterns that eventually lead to such events. Several pundits, such as Strauss and Howe, Williams Inference, and *Black Swan* author Yousef Taleb[35] – not to mention the canny investors who made billions on the stock-market collapse as portrayed in the movie *The Big Short* – detected the underlying shifts in the mortgage market and came to realize that the old order could not persist for much longer. If historians, economists, and investors are savvy enough to understand how the world around them is changing, why can't the same be true of corporate directors and managers?

CHAPTER FOUR

Confronting Reality

Larry Bossidy, former CEO of Allied Signal, and Ram Charan, an Indian-American business consultant, have an unusual definition of "execution" in their book *Execution: The Discipline of Getting Things Done*: "In the most fundamental sense, execution is a systematic way of exposing reality and acting on it."[1] Their view echoes Jack Welch, CEO of General Electric from 1980 to 2001, and Jim Collins, an expert on business sustainability and author of *Good to Great*, both of whom stress the importance of confronting unpleasant facts. The purpose of intelligence is to expose reality, no matter how brutal it may be. Yet most companies and individuals are not very good at facing up to the brutal part. In the mid-1970s, for example, Singer Company noticed that sales of its famous sewing machines were slipping. Management hired a new sales team to "push the iron." Unfortunately, however, the salesmen (and it's a safe bet that they were all men) did not bother casting their eyes beyond the four walls of Singer. Women had begun to work outside the home. They had less time for sewing. The sewing machine was doomed.[2]

Let's examine another more recent, high-profile example. Shares of Research in Motion (now Blackberry) peaked at $150 per share in June 2008. Just a few months later, in October 2008, Apple introduced its ground-breaking iPhone 3G. A key enhancement was the "app store," which offered users more than five hundred applications that they could easily download over the Internet. Almost overnight the industry's center of gravity shifted from hardware, in other words handsets, to software in the form of smart application platforms. RIM's stock hit a low of $6 in summer 2012, and the company has struggled to reinvent itself ever since.

What happened? As Jean-Louis Gassée, a Palo Alto venture capitalist and former Apple executive, told the *New York Times* in April 2011, RIM has "been caught flat footed. They've built a tremendous company; they are people with distinguished backgrounds. They are not idiots, but they've behaved like idiots."[3]

RIM would have done well to heed Michael Porter's definition of "strategic risk" as a function of how poorly a strategy will perform if the wrong scenario occurs. To effectively manage this risk, he noted, companies must consider alternative scenarios, even if those scenarios seem "unthinkable."

"RIM fretted about the very thing iPhone users considered irrelevant: network capacity. One of the great strengths of RIM's internal network system was its ability to compress large amounts of data, a service that reduced bandwidth use and data charges for customers."[4] The wireless industry had a long history of preserving limited bandwidth – because of the huge capital investment required to increase network capacity. RIM was certain it had no choice but to continue preserving bandwidth even as it applied more and more applications to the wireless spectrum.

But then the unthinkable happened. AT&T signed an exclusive agreement to distribute iPhones. "Three months later, in July 2008, Apple smashed the networks RIM wanted to conserve by launching the App Store. The online outlet was stocked with software applications that iPhone users, then numbering six million, could download."[5] A finger swipe could race cars through video games, book hotel rooms, and order food. Apple sold more than ten million apps in three days. Bandwidth conservation was yesterday's priority. AT&Ts networks were so clogged that customers began suing Apple and the carrier for dropped calls and other transmission headaches. The message was clear: wireless traffic was only going to get bigger. The answer was not conservation; rather it was bigger, faster, wireless highways, and the telecom companies would waste no time responding to the increased demand.

Ten years later, Blackberry is struggling to rebuild itself as a supplier of software and services focused on securing and managing the "Internet of Things." It has sought to achieve this with Blackberry Secure, an Internet of Things platform comprising its enterprise communication and collaboration software and safety-certified embedded solutions. Meantime, Blackberry's revenues have fallen from US$19.9 billion in fiscal 2011 to just US$1,040 million in fiscal 2020.[6] The number of employees has shrunk from 20,000 in October 2008 to 4,000 at the end of 2019. As of June 2020, the stock is trading at around $7, still a far cry from its $150 peak.

As Charles Darwin observed, "it is not the strongest of the species that survives, nor the most intelligent that survives. It is the one that is most adaptable to change."[7] Gradually we are coming to understand that to be effective in this world of rapid disruptive change, we need to learn more about how we organize and govern. According to Peter Senge, director of the systems thinking and organizational learning program at the Sloan School of Management at MIT, organizations that excel in the future will be those that know how to tap our commitment and capacity to learn at *all* levels.[8] Or as Arie de Geus, former head of planning for Royal Dutch Shell, said, "The ability to learn faster than your competitors may be the only sustainable competitive advantage."[9]

As the world becomes more interconnected and business more complex and dynamic, boards must ensure that their companies have the necessary mindset, beliefs, and culture to adapt to disruptive change. They must be on the lookout for signals that the world is changing, weigh plausible alternative futures, and not be afraid to challenge management to confront new realities. This is the essence of effective governance.

Founders Determine an Organization's Culture

Directors have recently started paying much more attention to organizational culture, mostly because they realize that their companies are having trouble keeping up with the speed and magnitude of environmental change.[10] Edgar Schein, professor emeritus at MIT's Sloan School of Management and the foremost expert on the topic, thinks of organizational culture as learned patterns of beliefs, values, assumptions, and norms that drive behavior. Company founders have a major impact on how their colleagues define and solve problems relating to the way they adapt to external forces and internal integration. Basically, the founders impose some of their own beliefs, values, assumptions, and behavioral rules on their subordinates; if the organization is successful, these become a way of life and a culture is born.[11]

Changing a company's culture is not easy. Continued success spawns two phenomena that complicate culture change. First, many basic assumptions become more strongly held and thus more deeply entrenched. Second, organizations develop values and ideals about themselves that are increasingly out of sync with their actual behavior. If the environment changes, some of those shared assumptions can become liabilities precisely because they are so strongly held. *In the maturity-and-decline stage, the culture often becomes partly dysfunctional and can be changed only through more drastic processes such as scandals that lead to mergers, acquisitions, bankruptcy, and turnarounds.*[12]

Culture evolves through the arrival of people with new assumptions, and through the differing experiences of various parts of the organization. Leaders have the power to enhance diversity and encourage the formation of subcultures. Alternatively, they can, through selection and promotion, reduce diversity and thus manipulate the direction in which the corporate culture evolves. But they need to bear in mind that the more turbulent the external environment, the more important diversity and flexibility become. Only an adaptable culture is likely to be a lasting culture.

Learning to Learn

A willingness to change course at both the individual and organizational levels is essential for corporate survival during times of rapid, disruptive change. This implies both a willingness and an ability to take the risks inherent in a less predictable future. Both change and learning require a fundamental shift in mindset. According to Senge, "learning organizations" are by definition responsive to change; they recognize that complex and dynamic systems are continuously evolving.[13] They continually expand their capability to determine their future by developing processes that enable them to map out a different future, and to implement strategies to achieve it. But even then, overcoming inertia and self-interest is hugely challenging.

The torrent of studies on change management is itself evidence that readying an organization for change is no small task. Importantly, "readiness for change" does not connote the actual process of change but only the development of disciplines that make an organization receptive to change.[14] According to Senge, these include systems thinking, personal growth and learning, adapting mental models, building a shared vision, and team learning. The bottom line is that organizations learn only through individuals who learn. Individual learning does not guarantee organizational learning, but no learning can occur without it.

Al Flood was able to turn CIBC into a "learning organization" in the early 1990s by driving home the message that the very top ranks of the bank were serious about change. Since CIBC is one of only a handful of large companies that has successfully completed a "learning organization" journey, its experience may be helpful to others thinking of heading in the same direction.

Four key premises underpinned CIBC's approach to learning:

1 The approach must be systematic.
2 The influence of senior managers is so critical that their questions and concerns must have priority.
3 Behaviors and habits must adapt to new ways of thinking and learning, not the other way around.
4 The effort must focus on performance, and it must be framed around specific business outcomes, such as consistently delivering an excellent customer experience.

From the outset, Al Flood recognized the critical impact that managers' mindsets would have on the success or failure of a new strategy. He also appreciated the value of highly skilled managers during a time of upheaval.[15] Without those attributes, the bank would not be able to produce the profits necessary to fund the transition.

Research over the past two decades has revealed three broad conditions essential for encouraging adaptability: a supportive learning environment, concrete learning processes and practices, and management practices that reinforce the right behavior.[16] An environment that supports learning puts minds at ease, values differences and new ideas, and allows time for reflection. Learning includes a willingness to experiment and test new products and ideas, disciplined analysis and interpretation to identify and solve problems, and education and training for both new and existing employees. Finally, managers who question and listen to their colleagues, encourage alternative points of view, and actively engage in learning processes reinforce the credibility of a "learning organization." The next two paragraphs show how CIBC met some of these conditions.

Building a successful learning organization requires that directors and managers exercise leadership. First, they must articulate a convincing vision and strategy so that employees appreciate that they are making a tangible contribution. Second, they must show that they can navigate the business environment and control the organization even in the face of complex change. CIBC addressed these issues through extensive in-house communication, including face-to-face "bear pit" sessions between executives and more junior employees. The culture was reinforced by special "strategic direction" issues of the bank's in-house magazine.

According to Senge, an organization's most precious assets are "its capability to build upon its lived experience, to learn from its challenges, and to turn in a better performance by inviting all and sundry to work out for themselves what performance ought to be."[17] CIBC instilled this culture by teaching its senior employees how to learn. Its systematic, three-element performance model (based on focus, will, and capability) emphasized the importance of excellent performance in the pursuit of business outcomes. This ensured that employees quickly became comfortable with the learning strategy and performance model. Holger Kluge's retail bank used this approach to create the Convenience and Imperial Service distribution models for branch banking. By setting different service and cost measurements for the two models, CIBC broke the traditional model of the same level of service for all customers.

While CIBC's approach is not the only way to prepare for change, it has been proven to be effective. As we will see in chapter 5, Jack Welch used a very similar approach to shake up General Electric.

Avoiding the Pain of Change

According to Michael Jensen, reluctance to accept change is another source of agency cost – in other words, the cost of conflicts of interest between the organization on one hand and individual managers and directors on the other. Change is painful, and pain-avoidance behavior has become so common in big companies that it makes transformation difficult, if not impossible, to achieve. Pain avoidance "causes people to become stuck, unchanging and unchangeable."[18] By holding onto preconceived ideas, individuals and organizations end up being substantially worse off. And to make these challenges more difficult to deal with, as discussed in the previous chapter, the biological structure of the brain generally makes human beings blind to their own behavior. For this reason, learning in these situations is both very difficult and slow. This pain-avoidance model led Jensen to recognize a second source of agency costs, those incurred as a result of conflicts of interest within ourselves; in other words, we want to do the right thing, but our own lives get in the way.

A willingness to change undoubtedly means accepting some short-term pain in exchange for long-term gain. Motivating individuals and groups to accept the pain and to move forward is especially challenging, indeed often insurmountable, in the absence of a crisis. That crisis may erupt as a result of a shock in the outside environment (quite rare) or the exercise of leadership within the organization (even rarer). In the case of CIBC, the huge write-offs on Olympia &York and other real-estate loans, combined with the internal reaction to being labelled "middle-management mush" by the previous CEO, were sufficient incentives for Al Flood to create and support the leadership center and its work to build a "learning organization."

Leadership – Creating a Different Future

When neuroscientists used sensors to locate brain activity, they found that the same part of our brain lights up whether we are thinking about the future or the past.[19] This means that unless we reprogram our brains, the almost certain future we face reflects the past. This appears to be equally true for organizations. Without a catalytic event or process, the almost certain future is no more than a continuation of the past, as *Stumbling Giants*, my book on the big Canadian banks, made clear.

Nonetheless, organizations can make choices; they can choose to strike out in a different direction. According to Roger Martin, former dean of the Rotman School of Management, a choice cannot be made until it is framed as a choice between at least two mutually exclusive and irreversible paths.[20] Furthermore, until a choice is framed as a choice, members of the group, in this case employees, will not truly engage in the change process, because they cannot yet understand the consequences of whatever choice they make. These assertions jibe with the two conditions of learning organizations discussed previously – leadership and control. Leadership is necessary to frame and make choices; control is essential to monitor the implementation of the chosen strategy.

One method I have used for more than two decades to devise strategy is a process known as "strategic choice structuring," developed by Monitor Group and Roger Martin.[21] It requires participants to frame the choice, brainstorm possible options, specify the conditions that must hold true for one option to be the right one, and design and conduct tests on the most important conditions before making the choice. This process addresses the two primary ways in which people try to assert control, especially in a threatening environment. They seek control by promoting technical ideas or barriers to shut down arguments they would rather not hear. Or they try to control the human element – making sure others are not heard, or not lobbying higher-ups for their preferred strategy.[22]

Defensive reasoning encourages individuals to keep private the premises, inferences, and conclusions that shape their behavior, and to avoid testing them in a truly critical fashion.[23] With that in mind, the third step in structuring strategic choice – identifying the conditions that need to be true for the strategy to be sound – forces managers to reveal their underlying assumptions and beliefs. Bringing those to the surface makes it much easier to search for information that confirms or dispels the previously identified conditions that would have to be true for the strategy to succeed. Transparency also makes it easier to monitor the condition for future changes.

Internally generated change requires bold leadership from individuals who are willing and able to create a different future from that foretold by the past. John Kotter, professor emeritus of leadership at Harvard Business School, defines leadership as the ability to cope with disruptive change – in other words, confront reality, set a new direction, and then persuade people to move in that direction. And since one purpose of leadership is to produce change, setting the direction of that change is fundamental to leadership. Many consider Kotter's 1996 article, *Leading Change*, to be the seminal work in the field of change management. In it, he outlines a practical, eight-step process for change management:

- Instill a sense of urgency.
- Create the guiding coalition.
- Develop a vision and a strategy.
- Communicate the change vision.
- Empower employees for broad-based action.
- Generate short-term wins.
- Consolidate gains and use them to produce more change.
- Anchor new approaches in the culture.[24]

The quality that separates leaders from managers is their ability to see and create a future other than the almost certain future dictated by the past, and a willingness to make the personal sacrifices needed to bring it about. These sacrifices include personal learning and growth, reformulating mental models, creating shared visions, and team learning – none of which can be easily or quickly mastered.

Confronting Reality

As Jack Welch, Larry Bossidy, Ram Charan, John Kotter, Edgar Schein, and many others have pointed out, change is about confronting reality, in other words, seeing the world the way it really is and not the way managers would like it to be. Leadership begins with confronting that reality head-on in order to generate a sense of urgency about the need to change. Although spotting disruptive change presents a real challenge, there are at least three ways that directors and managers can improve their track record – namely, by searching for anomalies, by scenario planning, and through dialogue.

Searching for Anomalies

Discovery begins with awareness of an anomaly.[25] One way of finding those anomalies is to actively search outside the company and its sector for contradictory information, irregularities, surprises, and other unusual developments that challenge the certain future that our brains have created. Anomalies are often early indicators of change, yet they can easily be overlooked in the morass of data that surrounds us today. Even when anomalies appear to be unrelated, closer examination often reveals an underlying pattern of change. For example, over the past few decades the suicide rate among middle-aged men has been creeping up. Meanwhile, in a seemingly unrelated development, drones and autonomous driving vehicles will be increasingly used to deliver parcels. This technological advance is reducing job opportunities for truck drivers, up to now the most common occupation for North American men. Could it be that the rising suicide rate is tied to the loss of these jobs? The goal in studying such anomalies is not so much to predict the future as to prepare for a future that represents a clear break from the past.

Nate Silver, an American statistician known for analyzing base-ball and elections, has examined the difficulty of looking into the future in his book *The Signal and the Noise*.[26] Silver discusses how we can identify a reliable signal in an ever-expanding universe of noisy and irrelevant data. The vast majority of predictions turn out to be wrong, often at great cost to society, because most of us have a poor understanding of probability and uncertainty. We are wired to detect a signal, often in the form of an anomaly, but we are all too prone to mistake a confident prediction for an accurate one. Alas, overconfidence often leads to failure. If we can improve our under-standing of uncertainty, our predictions will surely become more reliable, too. This is the paradox of predictions: the more humility we have about our ability to look into the future and the more will-ing we are to learn from our mistakes, the more we can turn infor-mation into knowledge, and data into foresight.

Corporate directors and executives need to scan the world beyond their particular industry – in other words, beyond their comfort zone – to help them detect anomalies early on, and then to capital-ize on them. "As with human peripheral vision, these (weak) signals are difficult to see and interpret, but can be vital to success or sur-vival."[27] Well-developed peripheral vision is especially valuable for companies operating in complex, rapidly changing environments, and less so for those in relatively simple, stable environments, since most disruptive change occurs outside industry boundaries. To understand the periphery, the board needs to ask open-ended ques-tions rather than focusing narrowly on competitive intelligence, as is usually the case when companies examine their long-term options. For example, the current threat to banks' payments business is not coming from other banks but from technology companies. Lessons from a company's and an industry's past are important, as are rel-evant changes in other sectors. Once the board has identified signals that it thinks may be relevant, scenario planning and other future-mapping techniques can help confirm its hunches.

Above all, understanding change should not be left to chance. Directors and managers have a responsibility to ensure the long-term well-being of their enterprise. Doing so demands a skeptical mindset that is always sniffing out risks and opportunities and identifying external forces that may have a bearing on the company's future. Yet most companies do not employ a strategic-risk manager with a mandate to look for anomalies in the external environment or to ponder their implications for the enterprise. If a company is very fortunate, and few are, the chief executive may – among her or his many other duties – have the clarity of vision to understand at least some of the forces bearing down on the business.

We can learn a lot about anomalies and predictions from the former Soviet Union army, which assigned an officer to every division to collect all the facts about a military campaign. This officer, nicknamed "the weaver," held the rank of a general. He (and it always was a he) obtained his information from field officers, foot soldiers, and spies, and from data received at division headquarters about geography, weather, political tensions, logistics, and local culture. Weaving all these sources together, he plotted the division's strategy. Companies also need just such a person. All too often, business information is disorganized, irrelevant, or inaccurate, dispensed from a fire hydrant rather than a carefully directed sprinkler. Furthermore, most managers tend to search for confirming information – data to support the path they have already chosen.[28] Seeking contrary information that upsets their preconceptions is far more likely to produce the facts necessary to re-evaluate a business or strategy.

As described in chapter 2, Williams Inference Global helps its clients search in financial markets for anomalies and patterns that have the potential to produce significant change. Williams began issuing warnings in 2005 about expanding bubbles in real estate, derivatives, shadow banking, and consumer debt, including mortgages. Its approach, known as inferential scanning, focuses on developments that are likely to affect the business environment – be they economic, political, social, cultural, technological, or regulatory. But hiring services such as Williams is only the first step in the early detection of disruptive change. More important is teaching directors and senior executives how to detect anomalies themselves, how to recognize patterns, and how to assess the implications for their business.

Michael Kami, chief planner at IBM and Xerox before writing *Trigger Points*, notes that the managers best equipped to deal with disruptive change are those who are intensely curious, observe events, analyze trends, and then translate all that information into opportunities. He recommends "razor blade reading" as a way to start.[29] Subscribe to thirty magazines covering fields you are interested in, and skim through them. Whenever you see a tidbit of information with a possible connection to your business, cut it out with a razor blade (or suitable substitute). Set up no more than ten files, each representing a key interest or area of responsibility in your business, and file your clippings daily in the appropriate folder. Review each file once a month. As disruptive changes start to make themselves felt far beyond your company, you'll be building a record of them. When you put all the bits and pieces together and review them, you should be able to see a definite trend, decide whether it's an opportunity or a threat, and start thinking about appropriate action.

John Stilgoe, a professor in the history of landscape development at Harvard, illustrates the point by showing his students some of his seventy thousand photographs, everything from street signs to storm grates. He has taken the pictures while traveling around the United States, often on foot or by bicycle, because cars go too fast for drivers to practice the art of noticing. Stilgoe's purpose is to teach his students to see well. "Most people when they learn to read, stop looking around," Stilgoe told CBS's *60 Minutes* in 2004. "I try very hard in this university, which selects students based almost entirely on how well they do with words and numbers, to teach them that there is another way of knowing. This 'other way of knowing' is observation."[30] In this way, students learn the power of accurate observation, enabling them to make more meaningful deductions and inferences. Companies could do worse than offer a course like Stilgoe's to directors and managers.

Another educator who has had considerable success in improving executives' perception of the world around them is Betty Edwards, an American author and art teacher best known for her 1979 book *Drawing on the Right Side of the Brain*. She encourages her subjects to draw exactly what they see. But to do this means circumventing the way the brain usually works. Our brains condition us to see what we know, not what is actually around us. By letting go of what we think we know, we free ourselves to see the world as it actually is. As Edwards puts it, "the trick is putting aside the knowledge that stands in our way."[31]

Scenario Planning

As Nobel economics laureate Thomas Schelling wrote,

> There is a tendency in our planning to confuse the unfamiliar with the improbable. The contingency we have not considered seriously looks strange; what looks strange is thought improbable; what is improbable need not be considered seriously.[32]

This confusion leads to deeply flawed thinking. If we examined our thought processes, we would surely recognize just how flawed our assumptions are. Schelling suggests that the problem runs even deeper. When a scenario is unfamiliar to us, we do not even think about it. Worse, we develop a sort of mind-blindness to it, and thus tend to resist it.

If we are to break out of this syndrome, we need to behave in a way that goes against normal human nature. In other words, we need to admit to what we don't know. This line of thinking was the genesis of former US defense secretary Donald Rumsfeld's infamous 2002 response to a reporter's question about weapons of mass destruction in Iraq:

> There are known knowns; there are things we know we know. We also know there are known unknowns; that is to say we know there are some things we do not know. But there are also unknown unknowns – there are things we do not know we don't know.[33]

The real problem arises when we choose to make no forecast at all, out of frustration that our knowledge of the world is imperfect.

One way of dealing with this problem is scenario planning, which aims to stimulate creative thinking as a way of helping an organization prepare for disruptive change. Participants start by trying to understand the major forces that might move the world in different directions. They map out a small number of plausible future scenarios, craft well-researched narratives to describe each of them, and then develop options to manage each one. Scenario planning is sometimes described as way of breaking through the "illusion of certainty" so that participants can rehearse the future and, in doing so, avoid surprises.

This process is useful because it forces us to reflect on the assumptions we make about the world, to address critical uncertainties, and to broaden our horizons. The purpose is not to come up with a forecast, because it will almost always be wrong. Instead, scenario planning draws a circle around multiple possibilities and prepares directors and managers to face the full range of events that might unfold. It also encourages them to ponder how they can nudge those around them even slightly in the direction they and their company may want to go.

Scenario planning has much in common with exploration and mapmaking. Like a set of maps describing different aspects of a new territory, scenarios provide us with a range of perspectives on what may happen, where pitfalls and roadblocks may occur, and where different paths may lead. Creating the map is as important as using it. Building scenarios allows us to explore possible outcomes rigorously and systematically, and the act of doing so can change how we see and understand the world.

Decision makers can use scenario planning to ponder aspects of the future that most worry them – or that should worry them – and to explore the different ways in which they might unfold. The scenarios provide users with a common language for thinking and talking about current events, as well as a shared framework for exploring critical uncertainties and making more successful decisions. The alternative scenarios all address the same important questions and provide insights into aspects of the future that are likely to persist. But each one describes a different way in which uncertain variables that shape the future may play out.

The Magic of Dialogue

Never underestimate the power of exchanging ideas as a way of discovering fresh perspectives and confronting reality. Dialogue is any serious form of discourse that strengthens mutual understanding as well as mutual respect and trust. Learning based on dialogue enables us to appreciate the viewpoints, values, and perspectives of others, to see where they are coming from, to "walk in their shoes." These attributes are precisely what company executives and directors need to improve their perception of what may befall their company and industry in the future.[34] When dialogue is conducted skillfully, the results can be extraordinary. Long-standing stereotypes dissolve, mistrust is overcome, and visions are shaped and grounded with a shared purpose. Most important, individuals previously at loggerheads with one another start to agree on goals and strategies.[35]

Dialogue-based scenario planning can work wonders in mapping out the future. It allows disparate voices and multiple perspectives to explore problems in an unusually productive way. It brings together different fields of knowledge. It reframes questions, eliciting fresh ideas across disciplines. It honors and respects differences of opinion, seeking only to define those differences clearly. It enables participants to explore plausible alternatives in ways that build enough common ground for them to move forward together.

As George Bernard Shaw observed, "Progress is impossible without change, and those who cannot change their minds cannot change anything."[36] In order to change our minds, we must first learn to "see" and confront the new reality, then prepare ourselves to act. Organizations do not change, people do. When enough people in an organization shift their mindset, envision a more desirable future, and begin to act to make that vision a reality, then organizations can start building the skills they need to broaden their horizons and tackle disruptive change.

CHAPTER FIVE

What Boards Should Do, but Likely Won't

Even when directors and managers are able to identify disruptive change, they rarely act on it. Yet directors have a fiduciary responsibility to ensure that the company is a going concern, to protect its assets, and to create long-term value for its stakeholders. They must exercise judgment on such critical dimensions as overall corporate strategy, risk versus reward, short-term versus long-term interests, effective oversight versus motivating management, ethical considerations versus market practices in different jurisdictions, and balancing the interests of competing stakeholders.[1] I refer to all these activities as *strategic governance*.

Strategic governance doesn't simply happen. In order for a board of directors to fulfill its mandate, it needs to rely heavily on the company's internal control system. But as Michael Jensen said in his 1993 presidential address to the American Finance Association, "By nature, organizations abhor control systems, and ineffective governance is part of the problem."[2] Directors do not have the time, resources, skills, or access to information necessary for strategic governance. Nor do most companies have an Al Flood-type "corporate center" or a layer between the senior management team and the board that can provide these resources.

Furthermore, businesses must be managed differently depending on whether they are in a growth phase, mature, or in decline.

According to Peter Drucker, a growth industry that can count on demand for its products or services growing faster than the economy or population manages to create the future. It needs to take the lead in innovation and needs to be willing to take risks. A mature industry needs to be managed to have a leadership position in a few, a very few, but crucial areas, and especially in areas where the demand can be satisfied at substantially lower cost by advanced technology or advanced quality. And it needs to be managed for flexibility and rapid change. A mature industry shifts from one way of satisfying wants to another. A mature industry therefore needs to be managed for alliances, partnerships, and joint ventures to adapt rapidly to such shifts. In a declining industry one has to manage, above all, for steady, systematic, purposeful cost reduction and for steady improvement in quality and service – that is, for strengthening the company's position within the industry rather than for growth in volume, which one can only take away from somebody else. For a declining industry, it is more and more difficult to establish product differentiation, as products in a declining industry tend to become "commodities."[3]

A business facing disruptive change is likely to wither unless firm action is taken to put it on a fresh track. As the experience of General Electric and a handful of others shows, and considerable academic research has confirmed,[4] getting out of a business is not only a viable strategy but often a necessary and attractive one. The resources needed for new ventures must be freed from the old business, whether through sale, joint venture, or closure (running the business into the ground). The tendency for managers to resist downsizing and restructuring underlines both the difficulty and the importance of providing appropriate incentives when such action is required.

Putting an entire company or even a single division up for sale is normally not an attractive option for managers or for directors, especially those with money, power, and status at stake. This is one reason why it is so important to have a "corporate center" with a mandate to keep nudging everyone in the right direction. The directors are ultimately accountable to shareholders for the long-term preservation of the company's capital, but they rarely have the time or the resources to determine the best approach. Chairs and chief executives cannot be expected to voluntarily consign the businesses they know and love to the auction block any more than they can evaluate their own performance and determine their compensation. Instead, the directors, as stewards of the company's assets, must ensure that there is a "corporate center" that keeps asking the strategic-governance questions: Are we in the right business? Do we have the right business model? Are we organized for peak performance?

I have identified three chairmen and CEOs who stand out for their perseverance in asking these questions and setting up governance mechanisms to provide the best possible answers. They are General Electric's Jack Welch; Ken Thomson, chair of the Thomson Corporation from 1976 to 2006; and Bill Anders, who headed the giant defense contractor General Dynamics from 1991 to 1993. These three leaders did not hesitate to sell businesses that were not well positioned for the future. At the same time, they made sure that adequate resources were allocated to business units that provided the best long-term returns to shareholders.

Ken Thomson did it because he took responsibility for the long-term preservation of his family's fortune. Bill Anders did it because he was incentivized to pick up the pieces in a broken industry. Jack Welch did it because he was a fiercely proud and loyal member of the GE family, determined to do his best for the company, no matter what the collateral damage. Sadly, very few other corporate chieftains have shown similar foresight or accountability.

Doing It Right

Only a handful of companies have responded effectively over the years to disruptive changes in the world around them. I will focus on the three mentioned above: General Electric under Jack Welch, General Dynamics under Bill Anders, and the Thomson Corporation under Ken Thomson. In the case of GE and General Dynamics, the board delegated responsibility for strategic governance to the chairman and CEO, who set up a "corporate center" to help him implement decisions. Strategic governance at Thomson was handled by

Woodbridge, the family holding company, which owned about 70 per cent of Thomson's shares. We will examine Thomson in more detail in chapter 7, as it is the best example I can find of corporate transformation – from a newspaper publisher, energy producer, and tour and travel agency operator to a nimble provider of specialized digital information.

Jack Welch, who was at GE's helm from 1980 to 2001, was one of the twentieth century's most admired chief executives. He laid the foundation for an effective governance strategy by challenging each one of GE's myriad businesses to show how it was going to be number one or number two in its industry, and threatening to close or sell it if it failed. Together with his vice-chairmen in the "corporate center," Welch spent a large chunk of his time allocating financial and human resources and massaging GE's culture. During his twenty-one-year watch, the value of GE shares multiplied forty times.

General Electric: Neutron Jack in Action

Welch stepped down from the top job in September 2001. His pride in the company's performance over the previous two decades seemed justified judging by the many accolades GE received. For the third year in a row, *Fortune* magazine named it the most admired company in the United States; the *Financial Times* went a step further, describing it as most admired in the world. And on the eve of Welch's retirement, *Fortune* named Welch manager of the century, noting that he had delivered an average annual shareholder return of 23 per cent. In his book, *Jack: Straight from the Gut*, Welch talks about the first time he appeared before Wall Street analysts. It was a bomb.[5] The analysts expected to hear him outline financial results and forecasts; instead, he talked about his vision: Growing Fast in a Slow Economy.[6] Those few words are very revealing because they capture the approach to corporate strategy and culture that Welch followed for the next twenty years – the same corporate-center structure that I was exposed to during Al Flood's tenure at CIBC.

In his maiden speech to the analysts, Welch quoted a letter to *Fortune* magazine from a planning manager at Bendix, one of the largest conglomerates in the United States in the 1980s:

> Through your excellent series on the current practice of strategic planning runs a common thread: the endless quest for a paint-by-numbers approach, which automatically gives answers. Yet that pursuit continually fails.
>
> Von Clausewitz summed up what it had been all about in his classic *On War*. Men could not reduce strategy to a formula. Detailed planning necessarily failed, due to the inevitable frictions encountered: chance events, imperfections in execution, and the independent will of the opposition. Instead, the human elements were paramount: leadership, morale, and the most instinctive savvy of the best generals.
>
> The Prussian general staff, under the elder Von Moltke, perfected these concepts in practice. They did not expect a plan of operations to survive beyond the first contact with the enemy. They set only the broadest of objectives and emphasized seizing unforeseen opportunities as they arose ... *Strategy was not a lengthy action plan. It was the evolution of a central idea through continually changing circumstances.*

Welch foresaw slower growth in the 1980s and believed that the winners in such an environment would be businesses that searched out long-term growth opportunities. That meant being the leanest, lowest-cost, worldwide producers of quality goods and services, or having a clear technological edge or an unassailable advantage in a specific market niche.

On the other hand, in cases where GE was not number one or number two, and had little prospect of gaining a competitive edge, the board had to ask itself Peter Drucker's tough question: "If you weren't already in the business, would you enter it today?" And if the answer was no, it then had to tackle Drucker's second difficult question: "What are you going to do about it?"

Around the specific goal of being number one or number two Welch wrapped three intangible values – reality, quality, and the human element. Reality meant seeing the world the way it is, not the way the board or senior executives would like it to be. This was not as easy as it sounded. It meant permeating the mind of every GE employee with the attitude that they should see things as they were, and deal with them the way they were. In fact, Welch went one step further, arguing that inculcating this concept of reality was a prerequisite to becoming number one or number two in everything GE did – or, if that was not possible, taking appropriate evasive action.

Welch tackled the other two core values – quality and the human element – through best practices, brain-storming sessions with executives, the Six Sigma quality program, stripping out layers of management, and a "vitality curve" to manage underperformers. Together these tactics would make GE more motivated, agile, and adaptable than companies a fraction of its size. By focusing on what businesses GE should be in and how it should organize them – in other words, devising an effective corporate strategy – Welch and his board created tremendous value for shareholders over two decades.

Welch practiced what he preached. By 1987, he had disposed of two hundred businesses and dramatically shrunk the company to conserve cash and redeploy it to the best prospects for future growth. GE walked away from investments in coal, petroleum, cable TV, aerospace, integrated circuits, mobile communications, small appliances, central air-conditioning, nuclear plant construction, broadcasting equipment, data communications services, and minerals exploration ... the list goes on. Welch recognized that some of these units were likely to be hobbled by stagnant or shrinking demand, while others were voracious consumers of cash that could be more usefully deployed elsewhere.

Yet GE also spent a net US$10 billion on 370 acquisitions on Welch's watch. It bought back NBC, which it had been ordered to divest in 1926 during the early years of radio and television broadcasting. It rolled out Genie (pioneering the firm's first online services), the CNBC business news channel, and, in partnership with Microsoft, the MSNBC pay-TV network. Most notably, GE drove into financial services, mainly through GE Capital, which powered the parent company's performance for many years.

By 1993, the transformation was complete, with a portfolio built around eleven market-leading, largely autonomous operating businesses. The corporate center then focused on driving the performance of existing businesses. Responsibility for business development and acquisitions was delegated to the operating companies. So long as they "made their numbers," each subsidiary was free to expand its business mix, thereby fostering innovation and entrepreneurship deep into the organization.

Welch also quickly streamlined GE's structure in a process he called "delayering." He believed that GE had too many layers of management; in some cases, as many as twelve between the factory floor and the CEO's office. Instead, he encouraged line managers to do their own strategic planning. At a time when the typical corporate manager had between five and eight direct reports, Welch assigned each of his senior GE colleagues fifteen or more. Few complained, as they learned that the extra pressure forced them to set strict priorities on allocating their time, and to abandon many wasteful processes. The only part of GE that Welch was willing to subsidize was a $75 million upgrade of the Crotonville, New York, management development center, because he believed that leadership training would be critical to the company's growth.

Welch's *modus operandi* elicited strong reactions, not all of them complementary. The downsizing process earned him the nickname Neutron Jack, after the bomb that could kill people while leaving buildings intact. A *Fortune* magazine survey of the ten most hard-nosed senior executives named Welch the "toughest boss in America." By 1987, large numbers of lifetime GE managers were taking early retirement, and Welch had installed a new top management team to implement his changes.

But Jack Welch was about more than slash and burn. He also paid close attention to productivity, introducing a new theme that he called Best Practices. The idea was to share good ideas across the company. He set "stretch goals" that pushed managers to reach ever-tougher targets. Management teams would come to the table with two plans: one that outlined what they expected to achieve, and the stretch goal that set the most ambitious target they believed they could reach.

Welch was also an avid fan of the Six Sigma quality program to lower costs and improve productivity by focusing on more stream-lined processes. Every GE employee underwent training in Six Sigma, qualifying as Green Belts and Black Belts; the program's terms and tools became part of GE's global language. For a time, Welch assessed managers based on a "vitality curve," a review process colloquially known as "rank and yank." Managers were forced to place their direct reports and staff into three key sections along a bell curve: the "top 20," the "vital 70," and the "bottom 10." High potential talent in the "top 20" were given plum assignments with more responsibility. The 70 per cent in the middle were largely left alone, while employees in the "bottom 10" were encouraged to find jobs elsewhere.

Together, these policies ruthlessly determined which businesses GE would be in, and how those businesses would be run and monitored. But Welch and his vice-chairmen wielded the ultimate weapon – allocation of resources. And they did so in a way that sought to maximize long-term returns to GE shareholders. The corporate center instilled its desired culture across the vast company through common processes and values. It exercised the managerial rights over strategic governance, while the board kept its hands on the control rights – ratifying and monitoring the executives' actions. Meantime, Welch, as both chairman and CEO, could keep a watch-ful eye on the board and the corporate center as they went about implementing his bold ideas.

General Dynamics: Winning the Peace

After the Berlin Wall came down in 1989, many US defense con-tractors found themselves on the ropes in an industry saddled with excess capacity. Some of the stronger ones were able to make bargain-basement acquisitions; others diversified into nondefense areas. General Dynamics chose a different route. It decided that it could best create shareholder value by seizing the initiative – downsizing, restructuring, and even liquidating parts of its business that no longer had any place in its long-term future. The company's new direction was guided by a fresh management team whose pay was tied to shareholder wealth creation. Certainly, handing out generous cash bonuses to executives amid widespread layoffs ignited controversy. However, from 1991 to 1993 General Dynamics' shareholders saw the value of their investment climb by US$4.5 billion, representing a dividend reinvested return of 553 per cent. The Virginia-based company proved how the right incentives can help shape corporate strategy, and that even firms in declining industries have hope for renewal.[7]

Bill Anders spent 1990, his first full year with General Dynamics (but before he took over as CEO), reviewing its strategy, as well as operations, markets, and financial structure. He quickly concluded that the company was headed for serious financial trouble without urgent remedial action.

The nub of the problem was that while many rivals had diversified beyond the defense industry, General Dynamics still earned more than 80 per cent of its revenues from the Pentagon. After Anders was named CEO in early 1991, he moved swiftly to streamline operations and improve profitability. Capital spending shrank to $82 million in 1991 from $321 million in 1990 and $419 million in 1989. Similarly, outlays on research and development were chopped to half of the $390 million spent in 1990. Trimming inventories and working capital helped bring down costs and improve returns.

A new vision for the future evolved over the next two years. The company sold its data systems unit to Computer Sciences for $184 million in September 1991. A few days later, Anders made two startling announcements at Morgan Stanley's annual aerospace and defense industry conference. First, he dismissed diversification as a viable strategy, citing a McKinsey study that claimed an 80 per cent failure rate for nondefense acquisitions by defense contractors. Second, he asserted that cash flows would be more than enough to fund the firm's liquidity and investment needs, and proposed returning "excess" cash to shareholders. Three weeks later, on 16 October, General Dynamics announced that its largest nondefense subsidiary, Cessna Aircraft, was for sale, and that it was studying all of its nondefense operations to determine if they should also be cut loose.

By the end of 1991, Anders was publicly urging the entire US defense industry to scale back in order to "rationalize excess capacity." He argued that only the top one or two contractors in a particular segment could survive the looming shake-out. General Dynamics itself would remain in businesses only where it could be number one or number two, and only if production volumes were large enough to justify dedicated factories. Anders identified four businesses that met these two conditions – military aircraft, nuclear submarines, army tanks, and space systems – and announced he planned to sell or close everything else. He told his competitors that General Dynamics was prepared to buy businesses from them or sell businesses to other parties in order to meet these "market leadership" and "critical mass" criteria.

General Dynamics emerged from these disposals as a much smaller and more focused company with just two core divisions, submarines and tanks. In 1993, it reported sales from continuing operations of $3.2 billion, just one-third of its sales two years earlier. Anders also continued to trim the work force. The payroll at year-end 1993 stood at 26,800, little more than a quarter of the number he inherited when he took the reins in 1991. The head-office staff shrank from 650 to about 200. In order to lighten the overhead burden on the remaining businesses, Anders announced plans to cut corporate staff to just 50 by the end of 1994.

The slimming-down process brought big benefits, and fast. Cash reserves grew from $100 million in early 1991 to over $4 billion by the end of 1993. The company used the cash to retire almost all its debt, almost treble the dividend, and repurchase 13.2 million shares. Finally, it returned $50 a share to shareholders in 1993 through special distributions. Shareholders gained almost $4.5 billion from 1991 through 1993, representing a three-year return of 426 per cent (553 per cent if dividends and distributions were reinvested in General Dynamics stock). And the gains were by no means transitory. Over the next decade the stock outperformed both the S&P 500 and the defense industry index by more than two to one.

The Anders strategy contributed to impressive wealth creation across the entire defense industry with a spurt of consolidation that returned over $10 billion to shareholders by early 1994. Numerous contractors strengthened their competitive position by focusing on a core business, shedding underperforming assets, closing offices and plants, consolidating divisions, lightening debt loads, and cutting capital spending and employment. The defense industry's returns from 1991 to 1993 (even excluding General Dynamics) were more than double the return on the S&P 500, highlighting the opportunity to create wealth even in a declining industry.

Some argue that Bill Anders could not have carried out this strategy without high-powered incentives. The new management team's compensation closely tied pay to shareholder wealth creation, including large cash rewards for increases in the share price. As General Dynamics executives grew wealthier even as they announced one wave of layoffs and divestitures after another, the compensation plan drew growing scrutiny, feeding a nationwide attack on executive compensation by politicians, the media, and shareholder activists. Nonetheless, General Dynamics managers have credited the generous incentives plans with helping to attract and retain top-notch talent and giving them the fortitude to turn a sinking ship into a speedboat.[8]

The Thomson Corporation: Stewards of Capital

Ken Thomson used his family's holding company, Woodbridge, to drive strategic governance and transformation at Thomson Corporation. Under his unassuming stewardship, the value of Thomson grew from roughly US$500 million when he took the reins in 1976 to US$29.3 billion at the time of his death in June 2006, making him the ninth wealthiest man on the planet, according to the Forbes 400 list. In an era infamous for egomaniac executives who squandered other people's money, Ken Thomson was a stand-out exception. He made a clear yet careful decision about how he would husband the empire that he inherited from his father, Roy, the first Lord Thomson of Fleet.

Ken Thomson was neither an entrepreneur nor a daring operator. Rather, he saw himself as a steward. His claim to management
fame was to hire some of the brightest lights in Canadian capitalism, notably John A. Tory, his long-time deputy chairman, and a
carefully chosen successor, Geoff Beattie, president of Woodbridge,
which holds about 70 per cent of Thomson Corporation's shares.[9]

In the 1970s the Thomson group was a conglomerate, spread
between newspapers in the United Kingdom and Canada, North Sea
oil, a UK-based travel agency, and a tour operator.[10] By contrast, the
Thomson Corporation is now a tightly focused electronic information publishing group of global reach, with most of its sales coming
from subscription-based products in the legal, financial, healthcare,
tax and accounting, and science and technology research fields.

The company hired top-notch managers and monitored them
closely; but more important, the board – headed by Ken Thomson,
who was also chairman of Woodbridge, and his deputy chair, Woodbridge's president – ensured that the company was in the right businesses. It made some wise moves. It decided to get out of North Sea
oil in the 1980s just before the collapse in world oil prices. A decade
later, Thomson Corporation sold its investment in the Hudson's Bay
department-store chain ahead of Walmart's march into Canada and
the erosion of the department-store model. It ditched its travel and
tour division before the Internet destroyed the travel-agency business. It sold its flagship, Thomson Newspapers, at the peak of the
market in 2000. More recently, it exited the textbook business to free
up investment for its "must have" digital information business.

What sets General Electric, General Dynamics, and Thomson
apart is that they succeeded in detecting disruptive change, then
responding to it in a wise but forceful way. Each applied the basic
rules of sound strategic governance. The boards of GE and General Dynamics delegated strategic governance – corporate strategy
initiation and implementation, strategic risk monitoring, business
unit strategic planning and performance evaluation, and culture
development – to the chief executive, who created a corporate center to help him deliver. In the case of Thomson, the controlling family chose to retain these strategic governance rights and hired the

resources to do the necessary work through their investment company, Woodbridge.

The problem in most other companies is that directors do not do the work themselves, nor do they insist that the company create the missing layer, a corporate center, to do the work, which they would oversee. This layer is essential to ask questions like, "Are we in the right business?" "Do we have the right business model?" "Are we organized for peak performance?" Without it, managers are inclined to do pretty much what they want, usually continuing to run the businesses in the manner to which they are accustomed, long after those businesses have reached their peak.

The System of Internal Control

As mentioned in chapter 2, Michael Jensen has noted that only four mechanisms can correct a divergence between managers' decisions and the optimal strategy dictated by a business's external environment. They are (1) capital markets; (2) legal/regulatory systems; (3) product and factor markets; and (4) the internal control system headed by the board of directors. Trouble is, the first three operate from outside and are unlikely to put the company on the right track in time to adjust to disruptive change.

That leaves only the board and internal controls to do the job. An internal control system must perform the following three key tasks if the board is to exercise effective strategic governance:

1 Initiate and execute corporate level strategy. This includes identifying new business opportunities, pursuing mergers and acquisitions, buying or building required competencies, and – last but not least – selling, joint venturing, or closing under-achieving businesses.
2 Oversee business unit strategy. That means guiding and controlling the planning process, capital allocation, and the appointment of business-unit heads.
3 Provide formal and informal mechanisms that act as the "glue" for a shared culture.

One purpose of the internal control mechanism is to provide an early warning system before setbacks balloon into a crisis.[11] To do this job, the board must ensure that managers are looking out for disruptive change beyond their usual comfort zone, and that they respond proactively once they have identified it. In conglomerates, the board often delegates such responsibility to individual business units. Research confirms that, with this approach, both levels of management (corporate and business unit) tend to put short-term investment returns ahead of longer-term sustainability. This may help explain the reluctance of these organizations to change course when they face disruptive change but before a full-blown crisis hits.

The system of internal control has three components: allocation of decision rights, performance measurement and evaluation, and rewards and punishments. Let's examine each of these in more detail.

Allocation of Decision Rights

The success of a business depends on how well it allocates the resources available to it. According to Nobel economics laureate Herbert Simon, decisions on resource allocation have four components:

- the right to initiate, including proposals for the use of resources and structuring of contracts;
- the right to approve, meaning ratification and veto power over implementation of decisions;
- the right to implement decisions;
- the right to monitor and measure performance.

While the right to initiate and the right to implement belong to management, the right to approve and the right to monitor are control rights. Control rights also include the right to evaluate management's performance in exercising its own rights. The separation of management rights and control rights is the key to exercising effective control at each level of management.

Accordingly, it is vital that control rights for key top-level decisions be exercised by the board of directors. To ensure that it fulfills this role, the board must take control of its own processes, composition, and agendas. This means that the chair cannot be the same person as the most senior member of management, usually the CEO. The board also has a duty to ensure that it has enough time and resources to fulfill its control role. In particular, it needs to have access to the information needed to effectively evaluate key corporate strategy decisions, namely:

- What businesses should we be in?
- How should those businesses be organized?

At most US companies, the chief executive does double duty as chair of the board of directors, making him or her responsible for critical issues like committee assignments; setting the agenda; and the quantity, quality, and timeliness of information provided to the board. Even in those companies where the two roles are separated, only about half of the chairs are independent outsiders. The others are former CEOs, founders, former CEOs of acquired companies, or persons connected to the company in some other way. By contrast, most British companies are chaired by independent outsiders, but a higher proportion of insiders sit on the board. Most Canadian public companies have separate chairs and CEOs, as well as a majority of independent directors.

Separating the chair and CEO roles is a necessary but not sufficient condition for ensuring effective control. If the board is to carry out its strategic-governance responsibilities it must have the time and resources necessary to do the job (as Thomson Corporation does through Woodbridge). If the board delegates these responsibilities to the CEO and corporate center, a control layer missing in most corporations, then it must be prepared to ratify and monitor management's recommendations. Otherwise, the key strategic-governance questions never get asked (or answered) and, like the frog in warming water, companies continue to operate as though nothing is changing.

Performance Monitoring and Measurement

If the board of directors is to do its job properly, it needs accurate and timely information regarding the corporation and its external environment. This means that, in addition to information on the company's performance, industry developments, and the company's positioning, the board needs to keep up to date on the following:

- developments involving various stakeholders, and relationships with them;
- legal and regulatory developments, and compliance with them;
- competitors, customers, main suppliers, and substitute products;
- general social, economic, environmental, political, and technological developments;
- leading indicators, such as customer and employee satisfaction surveys.

Directors can obviously never know as much as management about their company's operations, so they depend on the CEO to provide the relevant information. But the CEO has a powerful incentive to organize board meeting agendas and underlying information in a way that emphasizes his (or her) successes and avoids discussion of anything else. Unfortunately, the history books are full of boards that, for this very reason, knew too little, too late.

The issue is not just access to information. A board's ability to oversee management is also undermined by the fact that many directors do not have enough time, energy, or skill for the job. Two of the most astute observers of corporate boardrooms, Martin Lipton, a lawyer at Wachtell, Lipton, Rosen, and Kratz in New York, and Harvard Business School's Jay Lorsch, drew this damning conclusion on the way directors go about their work:

> Based on our experience, the most widely shared problem directors have is a lack of time to carry out their duties. The typical board meets less than eight times annually. Even with committee meetings and informal gatherings before or after the formal board meeting, directors

rarely spend as much as a working day together in and around each meeting. Further, in many boardrooms too much of this limited time is occupied with reports from management and various formalities. In essence, the limited time outside directors have together is not used in a meaningful exchange of ideas among themselves or with management/inside directors.[12]

Lipton and Lorsch estimate that an effective director needs to spend at least one hundred hours a year on the job. More recent analyses suggest that a director should devote at least 250 hours a year to any company with no significant problems. Including professional development, even this estimate is likely too low. In the event of a crisis, a full-time commitment may be needed. Yet very few directors are able to offer that kind of assurance, given that many serve on more than one board, and may even have other full-time jobs.[13]

Agency Costs and Incentives

Managers often pursue objectives that benefit themselves rather than being in the best interest of shareholders, a phenomenon known as agency cost.[14] They may be too busy or too risk-averse to respond quickly enough to early warning signals of disruptive change. Lucrative employee compensation is another way that agency cost can prevent growing, cash-rich organizations from moving in the right direction.[15]

Referring to Citigroup's residential mortgage business, Charles Prince, the bank's former CEO, infamously said in July 2007, "When the music stops ... things will be complicated. But as long as the music is playing, you have got to get up and dance. We're still dancing." Executive compensation structures all too often give rise to a situation known as "moral hazard," where managers reap substantial rewards from short-term successes but bear none of the long-term risk of their actions. They are thus incentivized to push for higher profits now, whatever the long-term costs to the company, its shareholders, and even, as the financial crisis has borne out, society at large.

Bill Anders, who successfully steered General Dynamics through a disruptive time in the defense industry, took a different and more enlightened view. "While other defense contractors engaged in a high-stakes game of musical chairs – hoping to be seated when the music stopped – General Dynamics pursued a strategy of offering its chair to the highest bidder," Anders noted.[16] As discussed earlier in this chapter, Anders and other senior managers were encouraged to boost the share price through a generous profit-sharing plan, stock options, and other incentives. Even so, Anders and his team used the wrenching post-Cold War period to set the company on a new course.

There are several reasons why managers who depend on salaries, bonuses, and short-term[17] stock options for their remuneration typically show little enthusiasm for painful restructuring even when such moves are clearly in the best long-term interests of shareholders and society at large. For example:

- Executive compensation is typically tied to the size of the company or the span of control. Economic theory suggests that compensation should be linked to firm size only to the extent that size is a proxy for the skills and abilities required for the position. Yet the link between pay and size has become the norm, partly because of widely used compensation surveys that use size as the primary, if not the only, determinant of pay levels.
- Executive compensation is also typically tied to accounting profits.
- Nonmonetary compensation – including power and prestige – tends to be a function of firm size and survivability rather than wealth creation. Managers involved in downsizing and layoffs risk being the targets of criticism from the media and their neighbors.
- Laying off employees and leaving communities is personally painful for managers, especially those with deep roots in the area.
- Managers often focus on survival rather than value creation. Many fail to understand the long-term benefits of selling or

winding down a particular business, even when this strategy is clearly in the best long-term interests of shareholders.

• Sacrificing resources to strengthen other parts of the business may ultimately cost executives their own jobs.

What Boards Should Do, but Likely Won't

So, what can boards do to help themselves and those around them confront reality?

First, they must ensure a clear separation between management rights and control rights for corporate strategy decisions. Those who benefit from running a particular business cannot also be responsible for determining whether the company should remain in that business.

Second, they must be well-informed about the world around them. Directors have a duty to constantly scan the external environment, looking for shifts that either signal trouble or present exciting new opportunities. This job is much easier if the company has a Russian army-type "weaver," or a chief external officer, as described by A.G. Lafley in chapter 2. If the company does not provide the board with these resources, directors should not hesitate to demand them.

Third, they must ask themselves a version of Peter Drucker's tough question: "If we aren't already in the business, would we enter it today?" If the answer is no, they then need to ask, "What are we going to do about it?" As stewards of the company's resources, the owners or their agents must be prepared to sell, close, or transform the business when clear signs emerge that a business is in decline, preferably before anyone else has noticed. They must then be willing to invest the proceeds in a more attractive business, or return the money to their shareholders.

The process for accomplishing these tasks is not a five-year strategic plan, nor the annual offsite strategy meeting. It is a continuous learning process, informed by dialogue with key stakeholders and supported by a corporate center responsible for strategy, governance, and advice on the long-term sustainability of the company. As we shall see in the next chapter, continuous learning and an awareness of little-noticed trends are among the disciplines that a new breed of activist shareholders is bringing to corporate governance.

Some Help from Outside

Directors would take their responsibilities far more seriously if securities regulators required them to consider strategic risk – the risk that the company is in the wrong business at the wrong time – and to report on the results of those deliberations in their annual information filings.

Accountants and auditors could also play a valuable role. The assumption underpinning generally accepted accounting principles is that the company being audited is a "going concern." But this concept is applied far too narrowly. If a company is not in danger of defaulting on its obligations within the next twelve months, then the auditors are unlikely to flag "going concern" issues. The fact is that sustainable capitalism is gaining more and more traction through initiatives such as the Sustainability Accounting Standards Board in the United States and the International Integrated Reporting Council, two groups that promote fuller disclosure of environmental, societal, and public policy changes in companies' financial reporting. The accounting profession also needs to embrace longer-term pressures and opportunities. One way of doing that is to take strategic risk into account in any discussion of "going concern" issues.

CHAPTER SIX

Barbarians at the Gates

By 2015, activist hedge funds had become a prominent feature of the corporate landscape, shedding some of their earlier reputation as avaricious and unscrupulous predators. And some of the most powerful among them were clamoring for radical changes across a wide swath of corporate America. Carl Icahn, Bill Ackman, and Daniel Loeb, among others, were feared and loathed in some quarters but celebrated in others. No one could argue about their firepower. Icahn Enterprises managed $32.3 billion in 2017; Daniel Loeb's Third Point had $22.6 billion at its disposal; ValueAct Capital, led by Jeff Ubben, $19.4 billion; Bill Ackman's Pershing Square $14.8 billion; and Nelson Peltz's Trian Partners $10.4 billion.

Although CEOs and boards dread the arrival of an activist shareholder on their doorstep, some acknowledge that these investors have brought about badly needed change, such as adding or replacing board members, raising dividends and pushing for share buybacks, forcing spin-offs, and even putting the entire company up for sale. Even when a company resists their advice, activists force their targets to evaluate and justify strategy, notably the appropriate scope of the business. David Beatty, the Rotman School's governance expert, succinctly sums up the interplay between activist investors and corporate boards: "Simply put, if boards were doing their jobs, there would be no activist investor opportunities."[1]

Activists adopt a range of tactics – from proxy votes and demands for board seats to full-blown takeover attempts. They also push for change on a wide range of issues – from governance and executive pay to strategic direction and excessive overhead. One of their most common concerns is the scope of the target corporation's business. Their demands typically include spinning off one or more units or even selling the entire company.

Private Equity to the Fore

Michael Jensen predicted in his seminal 1989 article "Eclipse of the Public Corporation" in the *Harvard Business Review* that "the last share of publicly traded common stock owned by an individual will be sold in the year 2003, if current trends persist. This forecast may be fanciful (short-term trends never persist), but the basic direction is clear. By the turn of the century, the primacy of public stock ownership in the United States may have all but disappeared."[2]

Jensen's dire prediction may have been a little premature, but it was still prescient. The number of publicly traded stocks has fallen dramatically. The drop can largely be blamed on outdated and discredited corporate-governance practices, which have failed to insulate business strategies from disruptive change or to manage conflicts of interest between managers and long-term shareholders. As noted earlier, Jensen's article has encouraged numerous institutional investors, like the CPP Investment Board, to shift a large portion of their assets from public- to private-equity investments, a strategy appropriately labelled "governance arbitrage."[3]

Jensen argued that the public corporation model is ill-suited to industries marked by slow long-term growth, where funds generated by the business outstrip opportunities to invest them profitably, or where downsizing – in other words, returning capital to shareholders – is the most appropriate long-term strategy. History shows that when an industry stops growing, the best use of capital is often to give it back to the shareholders so that they can put it to work more productively elsewhere. Almost every long-established business is under such pressure today, as change is forced upon it by modern technology, in the form of the Internet, mobile apps, cloud computing, artificial intelligence, blockchain, robots, and social media.

As Jensen saw it, the conventional twentieth-century model of corporate governance – namely, widely dispersed public owner-ship, professional managers without substantial equity holdings, and a board of directors dominated by management-appointed outsiders – remains a viable option for rapidly growing companies with profitable investment opportunities that exceed the cash they generate internally. But these very companies – Google, Facebook, Lyft, and Alibaba are good examples – have rejected the traditional governance model. Instead, they have issued dual-class shares that keep key decisions firmly in their founders' hands.

This is not necessarily a bad thing for shareholders, despite the governance community's distinct preference for an equal-votes-for-all share structure. A 2018 study by the Rotman School's Centre for Corporate Governance Innovation concluded that Canadian publicly listed family businesses, most of them with dual-class shares, had a significantly higher chance of long-term survival, more stable senior management, and lower stock price volatility than other types of com-panies.[4] An earlier study (figure 6.1) showed that Canadian family-controlled companies notched up a 7.7 per cent compound annual return on investment from 1993 to 2012, compared with 6.1 per cent for their peers, a striking 41 per cent difference over twenty years.[5]

Since activist investors also have a sizable financial stake in the companies they target, one would expect a similar result from their targets. And sure enough, their returns, on average, have so far exceeded market returns.[6]

Harvard law professor Lucian Bebchuk argues that we should applaud shareholder activism. Professor Bebchuk studied more than two thousand activist hedge-fund interventions between 1994 and 2007, using return on assets as a proxy for evaluating operating performance, and measuring companies' success in boosting their market value relative to book value. In both cases, Bebchuk found that performance improved up to five years after the hedge fund's involvement.[7]

Figure 6.1. Comparison 1992–2012: Family Firms Outperform Other TSX Companies over 20 Years by 40 Per Cent

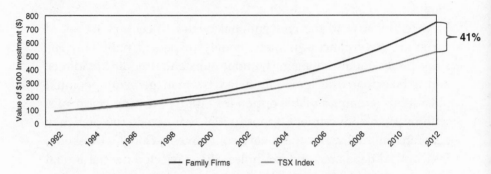

Source: Matt Fullbrook, David and Sharon Johnston Centre for Corporate Governance Innovation, Rotman School of Management, University of Toronto.

Friend or Foe?

Activists make a persuasive case for why their targets should either trim or expand the scope of their business. And they tend to exert maximum pressure to try and get their way. Even if companies refuse to take an activist's advice, they are likely to conduct a thorough review of their strategy and assess the best course of action more carefully than they might have done without the predator's intervention.

Arguments in favor of breaking up a company include the following:

• To facilitate accurate valuation. The sum of the parts is more valuable than the whole. Disparate business lines often make it difficult to value the whole company. They may have very different growth prospects, with a mature, slow-growing division obscuring the exciting potential of a newer, fast-expanding one. A spin-off may help draw out the full value of each business.
• To enhance management simplicity and focus. Divestitures tend to simplify businesses, enabling managers to execute a more

focused strategy instead of being distracted by the complexities of a diverse operation. Different divisions within a large company often have varying priorities and targets that can be hard to juggle within a single entity.

- To enhance analyst coverage. Analysts and investors are able to assess the strengths and weaknesses of a focused company more easily than a complex one. Academic studies show that analysts' research quality improves when a firm spins off operations peripheral to its main business.
- To enhance the potential to form new businesses. A stand-alone company is better positioned than a subsidiary to use its own, more accurately valued stock as currency for acquisitions in its field, or even to sell itself to others. Implicit in this argument is the belief that the business will fare better under fresh ownership.
- Lack of synergy. Some business units operating under the same corporate umbrella have no good reason to share resources or to collaborate in any other way. The combination may have made sense in the past, but external business circumstances may have changed, or some other rationale for keeping them in the same stable has passed.
- To return money to shareholders. The best use of a company's cash is to return it to shareholders, rather than supporting lackluster businesses or chasing other wasteful opportunities.

But there are also valid arguments against the spin-offs so often demanded by activist investors. These deals typically involve significant costs, starting with investment banking and lawyers' fees. Many companies benefit from shared activities and economies of scale, whether in purchasing or producing and selling multiple products. Similarly, a corporate brand covering several businesses can bring value by raising consumer awareness. Finally, a single business can be more risky and thus more volatile than a diversified one. A smoother earnings record improves access to capital markets and reduces the cost of funds.

Let's see how these arguments played out at General Electric. While Jack Welch may have done an excellent job of creating value for GE shareholders during his two decades at the helm, it is debatable how well he prepared the company for its longer-term future. His successor, Jeff Immelt, tried to address GE's delayed response to the Internet by, as he put it, "naming and claiming the industrial internet of things."[8] But after sixteen years of incremental change, time ran out. In 2017, Trian Partners, an activist hedge fund run by Nelson Peltz and Ed Garden, snapped up 1.5 per cent of GE's shares, enough to give it significant influence over such a widely held company. Trian replaced the CEO (twice), threw out most of the old board, and began shedding businesses. In June 2018, a year after Trian's first intervention, it announced that GE would in future focus on just three businesses – aviation, power, and renewable energy. By a twist of fate, GE was dropped from the Dow Jones Industrial average the very same month – the last founding member of the index to fall from that prestigious perch.

GE: Transformation: Underway ... but Nobody Cared

On 5 October 2015, almost two years before Trian Partners disclosed its investment in GE, the fund distributed a presentation in eighty-one slides titled *GE: Transformation Underway ... but Nobody Cares.* Although management had taken some bold steps to reshape the company, investors had grown tired of waiting for results. Trian believed GE could be worth $40 to $45 per share by the end of 2017, versus its 2015 value of $29. It made a none-too-subtle offer to work with management to help make that happen. However, the veneer of collaboration did not last long. Less than two years later, Jeff Immelt was forced out as CEO. The announcement said that he would also retire as chairman at the end of 2017, but he ended up leaving three months earlier.

Immelt started his tenure in 2001 at the tail end of an unprecedented bull market and in the midst of a global economic slowdown. His first day on the job was 7 September 2001 – four days before the terrorist attacks in New York and Washington. But by then, GE's market value had already shrunk by a third as investors digested the implications of Jack Welch's departure.

GE's mix of businesses in 2001 was mind-boggling: aircraft engines, appliances, capital services, personal finance products, industrial and power systems, lighting, medical systems, adhesives, sealants, automotive components, building and construction, satellites, retail services, communications services, motors, transportation systems, electrical distribution and control, water treatment ... and more.

Immelt's goal was to transform GE "from a low-margin manufacturer to a more lucrative industrial services company" that would thrive in the Internet age. He predicted that it would become "a top-10 software company" by 2020.[9] In one sense, GE was already service-focused. In his time as CEO, Welch had boosted services from 15 per cent of revenues to 70 per cent. However, most of that came from GE Capital, rather than GE's core industrial businesses.

Immelt understood the need to pare down GE's complexity. He sold off units representing 40 per cent of revenues as he redefined which businesses constituted its "core." Among other moves, Immelt pulled GE out of plastics, appliances, insurance, network TV, and nearly all of GE Capital; he put GE into and then pulled it out of security, water processing, and movies. On the other hand, he dived into oilfield services, software, and industrial 3D printing.

Immelt invested in GE's existing services businesses – such as aircraft maintenance and monitoring contracts and medical software and billing – where sizable players had an unmistakable competitive advantage. Infrastructure and infrastructure technology, he asserted, was "a $70 billion business that will grow 15 per cent a year for the next five years. That's a business where small people need not apply."[10] Confident that future growth would come from outside the United States, he shifted GE's focus to emerging markets like China, India, Turkey, eastern Europe, Russia, and Latin America. But refocusing the business mix in this way was a risky proposition, requiring patient long-term capital that Wall Street turned out to be reluctant to provide.

Immelt launched numerous innovation initiatives – with slogans like "cash entitlement," "simplification," and "imagination breakthroughs" – designed to improve productivity and streamline processes. He endeavored to take advantage of GE's size by demanding that subsidiaries share services like branding, marketing, supply-chain management, and logistics. The company ran two-thirds of these processes through its shared-services division, known as Global Operations, with the aim of trimming operating costs by 25 per cent a year.

Another innovation, the GE Store, was Immelt's way of cross-pollinating ideas for corporate renewal. The store's products, mostly based on new technologies, were used right across the company. Thus, GE's mobile power plants adopted processes originally developed for jet engines. The precision pipeline inspection team borrowed ideas from diagnostic imaging for healthcare. GE locomotive engines combined ideas from six other businesses to reduce nitrogen-oxide emissions by 76 per cent. Few other companies could rival GE's ability to disseminate its expertise in design, material science, manufacturing, software and analytics, and process engineering.

GE's biggest digital initiative was Predix, its cloud-based operating system for the industrial Internet. Using Predix, GE and its partners coded applications to gather and analyze data from machines connected via the cloud to help employees, customers, and operators make informed business decisions.

Under Immelt, GE doubled research and development spending to 4 per cent of sales, operated ten global research centers, and added more than three thousand patented inventions each year. In short, Jeff Immelt tried everything that strategy textbooks and consultants recommended to accelerate innovation and adapt to disruptive change.

But despite sixteen years of frenetic activity, the markets lost patience and the activist investors moved in. Although GE's directors supported Immelt's moves, they failed to recognize what many academic studies have pointed out: a corporate transformation takes a long time. If the organization does not start early, which GE did not, it is not likely to succeed.

For more than a century, General Electric had been lauded as one of the world's best-managed firms. Business-school cases celebrated its many management innovations, its strict strategy-formulation criteria, and the thoughtful details of its implementation processes.

But by 2017, it was the worst-performing company in the Dow Jones Industrial index. Make no mistake, Immelt oversaw some dramatic changes. But like many other boards, GE's directors failed to confront a brutal reality: the world was changing faster than their company. Even though Immelt had transformed the company from a classic sprawling conglomerate to a handful of industrial businesses, it remained a slow-moving behemoth. Most of its portfolio was in mature or declining industries that were being rapidly replaced by entrepreneurs with new, technology-driven solutions.

Jeff Immelt's successor was John Flannery, the respected head of GE's healthcare business. Flannery's abrupt elevation to the top job (see Appendix A) gave critics hope that GE was changing tack, reinstating Jack Welch's strict strategic-governance regimen. Flannery immediately picked some low-hanging fruit. He started by shrinking the board from eighteen to twelve directors. Within four months of taking the helm, he had restructured the top management team by coaxing some of Immelt's key lieutenants into early retirement. He grounded the corporate jets, slashed the use of company cars, and slowed spending on a fancy new headquarters in Boston. A month later, in November 2017, GE announced that it was halving its quarterly dividend on the grounds that it had been "paying a dividend in excess of our free cash flow for a number of years now."[11]

Flannery promised a restructuring that would generate $20 billion in cash. But a complete break-up of the company into separately traded units would be challenging. GE's business units were highly interdependent, enjoying the benefits of the parent company's low cost of capital, its efficient tax structure, a strong brand name, access to talented managers, a common software platform, and shared performance data. What's more, the subsidiaries were collectively liable for GE Capital's net $32 billion in debt and for the company's pension plan.

Within a year, Flannery was gone, replaced by Lawrence Culp, Jr., previously CEO of Danaher, another multinational conglomerate whose businesses included environmental services, dental equipment, life sciences, and diagnostics. Flannery was let go because he had not moved fast enough to satisfy the board. The new leader's priority was to lighten GE's debt burden, and free up more cash by spinning off the healthcare, transportation, and oilfield services units. These disposals, as well as several smaller deals, were completed by the spring of 2019, leaving GE focused on just three businesses – aviation, power, and renewable energy.

An Activist Success Story

Pershing Square Capital Management, an activist fund owned and managed by William Ackman, began its hostile assault on Canadian Pacific Railway (CP Rail) in September 2011. Its involvement with one of Canada's most storied companies will go down in history as a model of the benefits that hedge-fund activism can bring to corporate governance.

CP Rail's chairman asserted back in 2009 that the company had put in place the highest standards of governance. Indeed, the Canadian Coalition for Good Governance awarded CP Rail its Governance Gavel for Director Disclosure that year. In 2011, CP Rail came fourth out of some 250 companies in the *Globe and Mail*'s annual governance ranking. Yet, all the awards in the world were no insurance against unhappy shareholders.

Pershing Square began purchasing CP Rail shares on 23 September 2011. Within two months it had acquired 12.2 per cent of the voting shares, and it later boosted its stake to 14.2 per cent, making it the company's largest shareholder.

One of Pershing's first moves was to recruit Hunter Harrison, the hard-driving retired boss of Canadian National Railway, CP Rail's chief rival. On 6 February 2012, Ackman and Harrison gave a lengthy presentation in Toronto that detailed CP Rail's shortcomings. They told the assembled analysts and reporters that their goal was to achieve an operating ratio of 65 per cent for 2015 (down from 81.3 per cent in 2011 – the lower the ratio, the better the performance).

The board described these targets as "a shot in the dark," a clear hint of its disdain for what it saw as Pershing's ignorance of the realities of the railroad business. Relying on an independent consultant's report, CP Rail's chief executive, Fred Green, argued that Harrison's operating ratio was not achievable because CP Rail's trains had to contend with steeper grades and sharper curves than its rivals.

Undaunted, Ackman followed up with a scathing letter to shareholders in April 2012, disparaging the board of directors in general, and Fred Green in particular. According to Ackman, "under the direction of the board and Mr. Green, CP Rail's total return to shareholders from the inception of Mr. Green's tenure to the day prior to Pershing Square's investment was negative 18 per cent while the other Class I North American railways delivered strong positive total returns to shareholders of 22 per cent to 93 per cent." Thus, according to him, "Fred Green's and the board's poor decisions, ineffective leadership and inadequate stewardship have destroyed shareholder value."[12]

This time, the directors got the message. A few hours before the annual meeting, the company announced that Fred Green had resigned, and that five other directors, including the chair, would not stand for re-election. Pershing Square had triumphed in the proxy fight; all its nominees were elected.

With massive reductions in the workforce, an overhaul of operations, and a radical shift in culture, CP Rail today is a very different creature from what it was before the proxy fight. The main beneficiaries, of course, have been Ackman and his investors. By the time Pershing sold its last CP Rail shares in August 2016, the stock had generated a compound annualized shareholder return of 45.4 per cent, a performance well above that of both its main rival, Canadian National Railway, and the overall S&P/TSX 60 index. Over the course of five years, Pershing Square pocketed US$2.6 billion.

Lessons in Corporate Governance

The CP Rail saga teaches us that no matter how big a company is or what business it happens to be in, it is always at risk of attracting the ire of unhappy shareholders, especially those with the firepower to force change. In some ways, CP Rail was a sitting target, a widely held company with weak financial performance and a stagnant stock price.

Even so, the question remains: why did the board not see much earlier what became obvious very quickly after Bill Ackman and Hunter Harrison took control? Why would the board not call on independent experts to assess management's claim that it was impossible for CP Rail to match the performance of other North American railroads?[13] How could the board not have known that performances far superior to those targeted by the CEO could be swiftly achieved?

These questions expose a fundamental flaw of corporate governance as it has been practiced up to now: the gap between the information available to the directors and management on one hand and outside investors on the other. In CP Rail's case, the directors, following the norms of "sound" fiduciary governance, relied on information provided by management. They were willing to believe that the goals drawn up by management were adequate and challenging and were happy to lavish generous bonuses on executives for achieving these goals. But as Pershing showed, well-informed and aggressive investors are no longer willing to put up with such sleight-of-hand and conflicts of interest.

The massive amount of information now available on a publicly listed company and its competitors makes it possible for a smart shareholder to spot poor strategies and press for drastic changes. If push comes to shove, an activist investor will make its case directly to other shareholders in the form of a proxy contest to unseat board members responsible for the company's poor performance. If directors hope to hang on to their jobs in future, they will have to act like activist investors in ferreting out information and challenging management's strategies and performance.

Saviours, Not Sinners

As was noted at the start of this chapter, directors and managers all but issue an invitation to activist investors to step in when they are unwilling or unable to adapt to disruptive change. Outsiders have huge incentives to bite the bullet. Most hedge funds charge a fee – typically 2 per cent of assets under management and 20 per cent of any gains generated – that represents a far more generous payoff than the typically modest shareholdings of directors and managers. The large number of companies that could benefit from a shake-up, plus the governance arbitrage opportunity – in other words, the difference in rewards for directors with significant stock ownership and those without – are sure to keep the proxy battle pipeline full.

Activist investors often come under fire for focusing on the short-term: for example, cutting research and development spending and using excess cash to buy back stock or raise dividends rather than making investments that will secure the company's future. However, research shows that such actions may, in fact, not hurt a company's long-term value. Most acquisitions that involve diversification end up doing shareholders more harm than good. Companies typically sell off more than half of their acquisitions in unfamiliar sectors precisely because they have failed to generate a decent return.[14] A 2016 academic study showed that some companies in fact boost returns by curtailing research and development in favor of a more targeted allocation of resources to improve existing products.[15]

One private equity fund, Capital IQ, estimates that S&P 500 companies targeted by activist investors slashed capital investment in the first five years to an average of 29 per cent of operating cash flow, from 42 per cent the year before the fund's involvement. Meanwhile, the average outlay on dividends and buybacks rose to 37 per cent of operating cash flow from 22 per cent.[16] This may not be a bad thing if the business is in decline or about to head that way. Take, Starboard Value's 2014 assault on Darden Restaurants, the world's largest full-service restaurant group. The fund demanded that the board cut costs, spur creativity, and spin off real-estate holdings peripheral to its core business. Its intervention forced the directors to reconsider their longstanding approach to capital allocation, and they eventually agreed to give up Darden's control of its property-investment arm and change the way it ran its restaurants. By the time Starboard's CEO, Jeff Smith, left the board two years later, year-over-year sales had grown for six straight quarters, and the stock had soared 47 per cent as compared to the S&P 500's 6 per cent.

Bill Ackman followed a similar approach in his 2007 attack on Target, the second-largest retailer in the United States. After accumulating a 9.6 per cent stake and forcing his way onto the Target board, Ackman successfully pressured the company into selling off much of its credit-card business and setting up an investment trust to hold 20 per cent of its real-estate holdings. These actions may have succeeded in improving outsiders' perceptions, but they failed to address falling sales and profit margins. Target's inability to quickly adjust to disruptive change, in the form of online shopping and the 2008–10 recession, was the real reason for its poor performance. Ackman came on board either too late to address these issues, or too early to liquidate Target's other assets.

In my view, activist investors are forcing companies in mature or declining industries to address the brutal realities that confront them. The directors of many of these firms stubbornly continue to put their faith in businesses that are no longer growing faster than the population or the overall economy, when they ought to be spinning them off or closing them down. Putting a rocket under these recalcitrants is in the best long-term interest of all concerned – shareholders, employees, suppliers, and customers.

The trouble is that directors and managers have too many incentives to keep pouring resources into stale and dying businesses. One such incentive is the structure of their compensation. Many studies show that executive pay is more closely tied to a company's size than to its success. Also, the more the business grows, the more the social status of senior executives is enhanced. Rare is the CEO or director who wants to be remembered for presiding over an enterprise that makes fewer products in fewer plants in fewer countries than when he or she signed up – even when such moves may have lifted productivity and vastly boosted returns to shareholders.

Many governance experts, including Harvard's Michael Jensen, Ronald Gilson at Stanford, and David Beatty at the Rotman School in Toronto, advocate an ownership model that starts from the simple premise that an active owner will be a far more effective monitor of management than a bunch of directors with little accountability to widely dispersed shareholders. The dramatic expansion of private-equity and venture-capital funds over the past three decades undoubtedly supports that view. I have little doubt that Bill Ackman, Carl Icahn, Daniel Loeb, and their ilk are on the right track. But it is not clear to me that their swashbuckling approach will be effective in the information age. As discussed in chapters 8 and 9, we now need an entirely new, more inclusive approach to corporate governance.

CHAPTER SEVEN

Transformation: Easier Said Than Done

The management guru Peter Drucker has made the point that companies facing disruptive change have an option other than extinction or sale to an activist investor. Despite a host of academic studies and billions of dollars spent on innovation experiments, change management, and consulting fees, only a tiny handful of enterprises have succeeded in making the transition from one business to a completely different one. Among the many challenges of transformation is the difficulty of creating a strategy for an unfamiliar business. As Joseph Schumpeter put it, "Success depends on intuition, on seeing what afterwards proves true but cannot be established at the moment."

The scale of the challenge is highlighted by the work of Chris Zook and James Allen, both consultants at Bain & Company, who examined 123 companies in free fall or with potentially terminal problems. This fate most often befalls mature incumbents that come under attack from more agile insurgents, or whose business model is rendered obsolete by technology or market changes. In their book *The Founder's Mentality*, Zook and Allen identify three forms of disruptive threat:

• Product substitution, such as the shift from old-fashioned cellphones to smartphones.

- A shift in how profits are made in an industry; for example, the threat to traditional energy companies' prices from the rise of smart grids and energy exchanges.
- An entirely new way of delivering a product or service, as in the threat posed by video streaming to pay-TV, or the disruption of book retailing by Amazon's Kindle.

Zook and Allen found that more than half of the companies they examined were facing one or more of these three types of disruption; 16 per cent faced two disruptions, and a few were being forced to confront all three. In their experience, very few companies (they didn't name any) are able to survive all three storms.[1]

Those able to make the transition do more than just rejuvenate themselves. The founder, or someone close to him, manages to channel the company's original bold, ambitious ideas in a completely new direction. The trouble is that the directors and managers of most companies in declining industries have long forgotten these lessons.

Innovation: The Hard Truth

Clayton Christensen and his colleagues at Harvard Business School recently conducted a two-year study to find out why corporate leaders stumble in their efforts to transform a business.[2] Managers can learn numerous lessons from past successes and failures, but all depend on understanding the rules that govern business-model formation and development – in other words, how new models are created and how they evolve over time, the kinds of changes that can be made at various stages of growth, and what all this means for renewal and long-term prosperity.

According to Christensen, "Business models by their very nature are designed not to change, and they become less flexible and more resistant to change as they develop over time." In fact, the better a business model performs at its assigned task, the more interdependent its various parts become, and the less capable of change they are likely to be. The strengthening of internal bonds is not an intentional act by management; rather, it comes from the emergence of processes that arise as a natural, collective response to repeated activities. The longer a business unit survives, the more often it will confront similar problems and the more ingrained its approach will become to solving those problems. We commonly refer to this ingrained approach, whatever it might be, as the "corporate culture."

This pattern was so consistent in the Harvard group's research that they were able to portray the course of a business model as a journey with a predictable route – although the time that businesses take to complete the various stages of the journey differs by industry and circumstance. A business model starts its journey with the creation of a new business unit, then shifts to sustaining and growing the unit, and ultimately seeks to wring ever-greater efficiencies from it. Each stage of the journey supports a specific type of innovation, builds a particular set of interdependencies into the model, and is responsive to a particular set of performance measurements.[3]

These phases help explain why most attempts to alter the course of existing businesses end in failure. Unaware of the interdependencies and rigidities that constrain business units, managers attempt to impose new priorities or create a new business model inside an existing unit. Instead, companies wishing to pursue a different model would be well-advised to create a new business unit, rather than trying to change an existing one.

The most oft-cited examples of a successful corporate transformation are those carried out by a company's founder – Netflix, Apple, and Dell for example. They show that a founder can rejuvenate an organization while it is still in the formative stages. Although IBM's transition from a hardware provider to a services company in the 1990s is another often-mentioned example, it is not clear to me that IBM's success in the information age is by any means guaranteed. I have, however, found one well-established company that has been able to transform itself – arguably, the exception that proves the rule.

A Rare Success Story

As mentioned in chapter 5, Thomson Corporation is a fine but all-too-rare example of strategic governance in action. It shows that an effective corporate strategy involves constantly asking the question, "Should we be in this business?" Management presents its competitive strategy to the board under the assumption that the company is going to stay in the business. But the board's job is to help management understand the forces shifting the business's underlying profit model and act before it is too late.

Ram Charan and Larry Bossidy devoted a chapter to Thomson's transformation in their 2004 book, *Confronting Reality: Doing What Matters to Get Things Right*.[4] It portrayed the CEO of Thomson Corporation as a hero leader who transforms the company. Charan and Bossidy described Richard Harrington, named CEO in 1997 after running Thomson's newspaper business for four years, as a careful observer of the external environment who had started to harbor doubts about the long-term prospects of newspapers.

> More important, he had noticed that new players outside the industry were shrinking his customer base of advertisers ... As Harrington and the others in Thomson's leadership team studied their external landscape and business activities, they could see the outline of a whole new business model ... An electronic publishing business for professionals where the customer is ordering a product that's being paid for by someone else. The board and the family agreed that the risks were well worth taking in light of the opportunity to create long-term value and backed him enthusiastically.
>
> The proposal was not for the faint-hearted. It would take Thomson out of the business it knew best and at a time when it was at the top of its game, and thrust it into a new competitive environment, going head to head with companies like Reed Elsevier, McGraw-Hill, and Wolters Kluwer ... But in one sense the playing field in its formative phase was more level than it looked. Publishers were just starting to go electronic, and if Thomson could get in on the ground floor and build up rapidly, Harrington believed, it could compete with the best in the peer group. "It actually gave us an opportunity to not only transform our business," he says, "but to become one of the leaders in transforming the whole industry."[5]

This CEO-as-hero version of Thomson's transformation does not gel with my experience in the early 2000s when I worked with

Woodbridge, the Thomson family's privately held holding company. As a financial services analyst in the early 1990s, I took part in one of Woodbridge's grueling dialogue sessions with John Tory, then president of Woodbridge and deputy chairman of Thomson Corporation, and attended by various senior Thomson executives. They were exploring opportunities in financial services and had sought me out for my contrarian view of the industry's long-term prospects. They challenged my perspectives on corporate and investment banking for more than an hour, with penetrating questions that few of the institutional investors I regularly talked to had even considered. From what I was told, this was Woodbridge's normal approach to confronting the reality of its business environment. I like to think that I contributed to Woodbridge's understanding at that time of the evolving environment for corporate and investment banking and wealth management, so its senior executives could effectively oversee Thomson's expanding financial-services division.

In May 2005, when I was researching my PhD dissertation, I began exploring the question "Why don't companies change when it becomes obvious that their environment is changing?" An obvious place to start was by talking to John Tory and Geoff Beattie, both former Woodbridge CEOs, to try and understand how Thomson made its strategy choices. They provided some valuable insights.[6]

According to Tory, "strategy is a moving target and the company did not end up with the strategic shift it thought it was making. In other words, it didn't start out by saying: Let's adopt this brilliant strategy and then follow through." Instead, starting with small acquisitions and experiments, it headed in the direction of supplying information that professionals – lawyers, accountants, bankers, teachers, researchers, doctors – need to do their work. As shown by the accompanying timeline, the company made its foray into this space with a small acquisition in 1978 and continued in this way until 1996 when it made its first large acquisition, West Publishing Company, a legal information provider, for $3.4 billion.

The early experiments confirmed the business opportunity. The 1978 acquisition of Wadsworth Publishing gave Thomson its first taste of specialized information, college textbooks, and professional books. In the early 1980s, its UK arm already owned some professional publishing and trade magazines, which could be broadly described as information businesses for professionals. It experimented, long before the birth of the Internet, with an electronically delivered European legal-information service, which was successful enough to convince management and the family that a much bigger opportunity lay in wait. Throughout the 1980s and early 1990s, Thomson continued to add small specialized publishers to its stable, adding the capability to deliver the content digitally. It focused on the large North American market, recognizing from the beginning that the information business needed to be global.

Initially Thomson did not have much money to invest in new ventures, so Woodbridge (in effect, the Thomson family) financed the initial investments in North American electronic publishing. Woodbridge was concerned about the risky nature of the new venture, and whether it was appropriate for shareholders of Thomson Newspapers. It was only several years later, when it became clear just how appropriate it was, that the family rolled the electronic publishing business into the publicly listed Thomson Corporation.[7]

Meantime, Woodbridge decided to sell Thomson Travel, not because high oil prices and the related decline in consumer spending reduced the profitability of its airline business, but because it wanted the money to pursue its new strategy of building an electronic-publishing behemoth. The story was similar with Thomson's North Sea oil interests, even though they were producing strong cash flows. Woodbridge did not like the fact that it did not have control over either the operations or oil prices.

Once Woodbridge was convinced that there was a viable strategy in the specialized information and publishing business, it was determined to lay its hands on the cash needed to move in that direction, rather than continuing to grow slowly with the cash flow from its North Sea oil and travel businesses. It took until 1999, twenty years after its first investment in electronic information, for Thomson to free up enough capital to make the acquisitions necessary to make a full commitment to information publishing, including the purchase of West Publishing in 1996.

Woodbridge did not want to invest in newspapers in North America because International Thomson (the name of one of its public companies at the time) would be competing with the family's other public company, Thomson Newspapers. Woodbridge also considered cable TV, but decided it was too capital intensive. But it did like cable's subscription model, which Woodbridge was confident could also be applied to business information.

The seismic shift did not happen overnight but slowly over two decades, starting in 1978 with the first acquisition in North America and culminating in the 2000 sale of Thomson Newspapers. (See Appendix B for details.) The new direction was a collaborative effort between Thomson management and the family owners. Although management was part of the decision-making process, it was Woodbridge that made the decisions to sell North Sea oil, Thomson Travel, and, ultimately Thomson Newspapers. Management was too committed to the old businesses to sell them at a time when their profits were still growing handsomely.

Thomson's experience explains how owners and those who represent them are able to make tough decisions when confronted with disruptive change in the world around them. They dare not shy away from drastic action, including getting out of familiar, even still-profitable, businesses to free up resources for new ones with a better chance of long-term success.

Much the same applied to General Dynamics under Bill Anders, as discussed in chapter 4. Prior to Anders's recruitment, the Crown family had lifted its equity stake to 22 per cent. However, Anders negotiated a contract that gave him complete independence. He realized the pressures involved in working for a dominant shareholder and wanted to be free from those constraints. His employment agreement also ensured that he would be comfortably well off even if he retired on the very day he showed up for work at General Dynamics. This was the kind of independence he felt necessary to make the changes that were required.[8]

Hold the Applause for IBM

IBM is often cited as an example of transformation in the face of disruptive changes in its external environment. In my view, however, it is not entirely clear that the kudos is well deserved, or even whether the Armonk, New York-based giant will survive the continuing shake-out among technology companies.

IBM has its origins in the consolidation of several companies that worked to automate routine business transactions in the early twentieth century. One, which leased record-keeping devices such as Hollerith punch cards and card readers to government bureaus and insurance agencies, became the Computing-Tabulating-Recording Company (CTR). Thomas J. Watson bought the company in 1924, giving it the name International Business Machines. From there, IBM expanded over the next half-century into electric typewriters, various other office machines, and, most notably, mainframe computers. Watson was a salesman, and he concentrated on building a highly motivated, well-paid sales force that could help clients adapt to unfamiliar new technology. His motto was THINK, and customers were advised not to "fold, spindle, or mutilate" the delicate cardboard punch cards. IBM's first experiments with computers in the 1940s and 1950s were modest advances on the card-based system. Its great breakthrough came in the 1960s with its Model 360 mainframe. IBM offered a full range of hardware, software, and service agreements, so that users would remain loyal as their needs grew. Since most software was custom-written by in-house programmers, and would run on only one brand of computer, it was too expensive to switch brands. Brushing off clone makers, and facing down a federal anti-trust suit, IBM sold reputation and security as well as hardware, and was one of the most admired American corporations of the 1970s and 1980s.[9]

But the late 1980s and early 1990s were cruel to Big Blue. Its losses topped $8 billion in 1993 as it failed to adjust quickly enough to the personal computer revolution. Desktop machines offered the computing power that users needed and were vastly easier to operate than multi-million-dollar mainframes. IBM did introduce a popular line of microcomputers, which attracted a host of competitors.

Clone makers undersold IBM, and the bulk of the profits went to chip makers like Intel or software houses like Microsoft.

In April 1993, IBM hired Louis Gerstner, Jr., as its new CEO, the first leader from outside its ranks since 1914. Gerstner had been chairman and CEO of the consumer products giant RJR Nabisco for four years, and had previously spent eleven years as a top executive at American Express. Gerstner brought with him a customer-oriented mindset and strategic-thinking expertise honed through years as a management consultant at McKinsey & Company.

Recognizing that his most urgent priority was to stabilize the company, he took quick and dramatic action, putting the most serious problems at the top of his list. Early moves included a renewed commitment to the mainframe and selling the defense-related systems-integration-applications division to replenish the company's cash coffers. Among many cost-saving measures, he took an ax to the workforce, which reached a low of 220,000 employees in 1994, half the number in 1992. Most important, Gerstner decided to reverse earlier moves to spin off business units into separate companies. He recognized that one of IBM's enduring strengths was its ability to provide integrated computer systems rather than just supplying individual parts or components. Splitting up the company would have destroyed that advantage.

These early steps worked. IBM was in the black by 1994, turning a profit of $3 billion. But stabilization was not Gerstner's endgame; he knew that he had to restore IBM's once-vaunted reputation. To do that, he needed to devise a winning business strategy. Over the next decade, he crafted a business model that distanced IBM from low-margin commodity businesses and focused on added-value opportunities. To that end, the company sold off its interests in personal printers and hard drives, among others. It launched a global services arm that rapidly became a leading technology integrator. Crucial to this success was the decision to work with whatever technology was most suitable for the client, even if it came from an IBM rival. IBM augmented this services business with the 2002 acquisition of PricewaterhouseCoopers' consultancy division for US$3.5 billion.

Instinctively, Gerstner followed the approach described by Zook and Allen to reverse a free fall caused by an attack from agile new players, namely, return to the strategy that had made the company successful in the first place. One of the first decisions he made was to reverse the decision to split IBM into smaller business units. As a former customer, Gerstner appreciated the value and realized the uniqueness of IBM's ability to offer its customers an integrated solution. Focusing on the "core of the core business," IBM rebuilt its sales force into integrated solutions providers, sold its noncore businesses, and enhanced its network computing skills to embrace the Internet. This transformation served Big Blue well for nearly twenty years.

More recently however, IBM appears once again to have slipped behind. Revenues tumbled from $107 billion in 2011 to $80 billion in 2018, a drop of 25 per cent. By contrast, rivals like Microsoft, Oracle, and Cisco continued to post strong growth. What's more, IBM's net income fell from $17 billion in 2012 to $6 billion in 2017. Clearly, another shot in the arm is called for. Quite possibly IBM's initial business model has run its course, and the time has come to shift to an entirely new business model, as Thomson Corporation did.

Disruptive Innovation at Work

Clayton Christensen's theory of disruptive innovation, discussed in chapter 3, was initially a statement about correlation. Empirical findings showed that incumbents outperformed new entrants in sustained innovation but underperformed when the innovation was forced on them by outside events. The reason for this correlation was not immediately clear but, one by one, the elements of the theory fell into place.

First, researchers realized that a company's propensity for deep-rooted change is profoundly influenced by feedback from its customers, who provide the resources that it needs to survive. In other words, successful incumbents (sensibly) listen to their customers, and concentrate on the innovations most likely to sustain those relationships. Researchers also arrived at a second insight: incumbents' focus on existing customers becomes cast in stone as tried-and-trusted internal processes make it difficult for even senior managers to shift investment in more imaginative but risky directions. For example, interviews with managers of established companies in the old disk-drive industry revealed that resource-allocation processes gave priority to sustaining innovations that produced high margins and targeted large markets with well-known customers. At the same time, however, these processes inadvertently – but unmistakably – starved disruptive innovations that were targeted at smaller, more poorly defined markets.

Those two insights help explain why incumbents rarely respond effectively (if at all) to disruptive innovation, but they do not tell us why new entrants eventually but inexorably move to challenge incumbents. It turns out that the same forces discouraging incumbents from allocating resources to counter early-stage disruptions also draw newcomers into disrupting existing markets.

The fact is that the seemingly least attractive customers and markets are often pursued not by a lone would-be disrupter but by several insurgents whose products are simpler, more convenient, or less costly than incumbents' offerings. Meanwhile, the entrenched players keep prices high, allowing many of the newcomers to enjoy profitable growth. But that happy situation does not last long. As incumbents (rationally, but mistakenly) cede the low-hanging fruit, they remove the price umbrella, and price-based competition among the new entrants intensifies. Some newcomers will flounder, but the smart ones – the true disrupters – will improve their products, enabling them to compete on an ever-widening front against higher-cost established competitors. The disruptive effect drives every player – incumbents as well as newcomers – to focus on the most attractive customers.

With this explanation in hand, the theory of disruptive innovation has gone beyond simple correlation to a theory of cause-and-result as well. The key elements of the theory have been studied and validated in many industries, including retail, computers, printing, motorcycles, cars, semiconductors, cardiovascular surgery, management education, financial services, management consulting, cameras, communications, and computer-aided design software.

Christensen's conclusion clearly supports Schumpeter's theory of creative destruction, describing how disruptive entrepreneurs ultimately replace incumbents. To ensure that the incumbent survives, its directors must be on the lookout for these disruptors and begin a process of transformative change as soon as it becomes clear that the threat is real.

A New Path to Corporate Transformation

After several years of developing strategies that were never implemented, I realized that the only strategy that ever does get implemented is the one developed by those who have to implement it. This means creating a process for strategy development and implementation that puts responsibility for change in the hands of the stakeholders. The role of the board of directors is to recognize the need for transformative change and trigger (or catalyze) the process, trusting that the stakeholders will offer a workable solution. The board's role is then to ensure that the necessary change happens.

When our task force on Canada's payments system started work in 2010, a wave of new technology, in the form of smartphones, was about to turn the banking landscape upside down. Thanks to the big banks, Canada's payments system had been a world leader, but it was rapidly falling behind. Yet the incumbents – banks and networks like Visa and MasterCard – saw no reason to change. I knew, based on my experience at CIBC and with other financial services and technology clients, that real transformation would require a different process that would encourage players in the payments business to be more receptive to change.

Effective leadership and governance in the information age depend less on a traditional command-and-control approach than on creating shared meanings and frameworks. Rapid disruptive change requires organizational agility and continuous learning, not lengthy post-mortems of past mistakes. A process of deeper learning and action encourages all stakeholders to move unmistakably forward. Leadership in the information age is about bringing people

Figure 7.1. The Catalytic-Governance Process

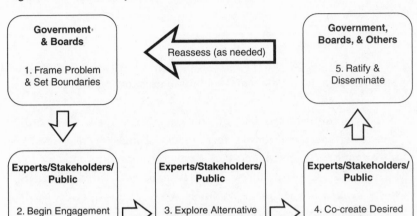

together to help them make sense of what they are doing so that everyone feels committed, both to the process and to the ultimate goal.

I call that process catalytic governance (see figure 7.1).

The point about catalytic governance is that it encourages and enables diverse groups of stakeholders to work through issues; find common ground; construct shared mental maps, norms, and expectations; and act accordingly. This foundation is essential for tackling transformation in an era of unusually volatile and far-reaching change.

The power of catalytic governance lies in the combination of dialogue, scenarios, and action. Dialogue is important. Scenarios are important. But traction comes when people roll up their sleeves and do the work. That is what makes it stick. The key to success is to recognize that catalytic governance does not replace debate, advocacy, negotiation, or decision making – it precedes them.

The core role of the board of directors – to ensure that the actions taken are in the best long-term interest of the corporation – is indispensable in this process. What changes is not these fundamental responsibilities but how the board can carry them out effectively in the information age.

Catalytic governance comprises five stages, as shown in the following chart:

Step 1: Frame the problem and set boundaries for solutions.

Before venturing down the catalytic-governance road, the board must determine the need for transformative change. It is responsible for framing the problem and the agenda, laying out the process to be followed, identifying the stakeholders to be included, and setting the boundaries for acceptable solutions. Above all, the directors need to put themselves in a position where they trust the process and are willing to place the onus on stakeholders to deliver an acceptable outcome.

Step 2: Launch engagement and dialogue.

A wide range of stakeholders must be engaged, with the ground rules of dialogue and consultation embedded from the outset. The board needs to ensure that all key viewpoints are sought; these are likely to include customers, suppliers, investors, employees, and partners. The stakeholders should be a microcosm of the issue at hand, not just representatives of particular interests. In a true dialogue, participants need to be free to speak for themselves, not as representatives.

When engaging stakeholders face-to-face, it is important to have a manageable number of participants. They should be drawn from a wide spectrum of backgrounds and sectors, represent a range of viewpoints, and include many who are not afraid to shake up the old order. All must be willing to work with others to develop a better understanding of the issue at hand and to explore all potential solutions. What's more, the recruitment process should be designed to continually broaden engagement beyond the core group, as needed.

Step 3: Explore alternative perspectives and future scenarios.

Participants in catalytic governance make a point of exploring a variety of perspectives in detail, as well as alternative scenarios for the future. This enables each of them to appreciate other points of view and to start seeing the limitations of their own arguments. Taking multiple viewpoints into account creates a richer view of both the present and the future.

Step 4: Jointly create the desired future.

Those stakeholders who are prepared to act must define their desired future and develop practical steps to realize that future. Often this requires what I call "action learning" – starting with small, experimental steps, and learning from the results. Again, to be effective, the stakeholder group must include individuals with the authority to bring about change, and the willingness to make it happen.

Step 5: Ratify and disseminate the desired future.

Directors must play a leading role, first by ratifying and disseminating the results of the catalytic-governance process, then by implementing the emerging strategy, and finally by monitoring the results. This step does not mark a once-and-for-all end-point; rather, it is the start of the next round of action learning.

Catalytic governance requires effective leadership and oversight from the board of directors. It was not until I oversaw the process at CPA Canada "to reimagine the accounting profession for the information age" that I realized the importance of leadership and oversight. Because insiders often cannot see the forest for the trees, it is up to the directors to launch, or catalyze, transformative change. Their leadership is necessary to identify the disruptive forces circling a business, to build awareness and understanding, and to create a shared vision of a desirable future. Just as important, board oversight is essential to ensure the implementation of the desired future.

Leadership in the Information Age

What is leadership? Although more books have been written about this than any other business topic, we still do not have a clear understanding of leadership and how to exercise it. Alex Haslam, a senior fellow at the Canadian Institute for Advanced Research, and his co-authors have come closest, in my opinion, in their 2011 book, *The New Psychology of Leadership: Identity, Influence and Power:*

> Leadership, for us, is not simply about getting people to do things. It is about getting them to *want* to do things. Leadership, then, is about shaping beliefs, desires, and priorities. It is about achieving influence, not securing compliance. Leadership therefore needs to be distinguished from such things as management, decision-making and authority. These are all important and they are all implicated in the leadership process. But, from our definition, good leadership is not determined by competent management, skilled decision-making, or accepted authority in and of themselves. The key reason for this is that these things do not necessarily involve winning the hearts and minds of others or harnessing their energies and passions. Leadership always does.
>
> ... if one can inspire people to want to travel in a given direction, then they will continue to act even in the absence of the leader. If one is seen as articulating what people want to do, then each act of persuasion increases the credibility of the leader and makes future persuasion both more likely and easier to achieve. In other words, instead of being self-depleting, true leadership is self-regenerating. And it is this remarkable – almost alchemic – quality that makes the topic of leadership so fascinating and important.[10]

The authors go on to argue that leaders' success depends on the degree to which they define themselves in terms of shared group membership, and hence engage with each other as a cohesive group. It is precisely because leaders stop thinking in terms of what divides them as individuals and focus instead on what unites them as group members that makes it possible for them to lead and their followers to follow. This approach gives the entire group a sense of direction and purpose.

Sound leadership is essential to catalytic governance. The leader's role is to help the group identify threats and opportunities and to work as a member of the group to find a way forward. But, as Haslam notes, "Without the support and sweat of followers, the words of leaders are nothing."[11] To be effective, leaders must do three things well – reflection, representation, and realization. Reflection requires the leader to get to know the group that he or she wishes to lead. That means understanding its history, culture, and identity and working out how it relates to other groups. Effective representation requires that leaders come up with proposals consistent with the group's values and aspirations. Realization means achieving the group's goals and creating a milieu that reflects the group's social environment.[12]

Catalytic governance is designed to achieve these leadership goals. Step 2 – dialogue and engagement – brings together a diverse group of stakeholders with the goal of finding common ground and exploring the challenges and opportunities of the future. Step 3 – exploring alternative futures – focuses the group on the future, in order to develop a way forward that all members desire and are prepared to work together to achieve.

In conclusion, leadership by the board of directors is essential to catalyze a transformation, and a transformative process is necessary for the board to deliver sound leadership. This symbiotic relationship between leadership and governance was articulated thirty-five years ago in a prescient work by statesman and academic Harlan Cleveland in his seminal article "The Twilight of Hierarchy." In the information age, he said, "Decision-making proceeds not by the flow of recommendations up and orders down, but by development of a shared sense of direction among those who must form the parade, if there is going to be a parade."[13]

The Value of Oversight

In the absence of an effective governance and oversight process, implementing the conclusions of the Payments Task Force and the CPA Canada Foresight project took far longer than I would have liked. Boards play a leading role in creating a desired future, first by ratifying and disseminating the result of the catalytic-governance process, and then by acting and encouraging action on the emerging strategy (including changing senior executives if necessary) and monitoring the results. Because the Finance Ministry and the CPA Canada board of directors were not engaged in the process, they did not feel the sense of urgency created by the group and were willing to accept a much slower approach to implementation than the pace demanded by the changing external environment. Like GE, they are headed in the right direction but may not get there before time runs out.

One of the board's first priorities should be to reallocate resources from the old business model to the new one. As discussed in chapter 4, boards are typically skittish about taking this step. At Thomson Corporation, it was the family holding company, Woodbridge, that not only found the funds needed to experiment with the electronic publishing business but continued to provide whatever was needed until it was confident that electronic publishing was a business worth having. Only then did Woodbridge roll the investment into the publicly listed Thomson Corporation.

With no clear accountability for their company's long-term survival, most directors prefer to look the other way, avoiding any attempt to understand the forces bearing down on them, or any action to counter the looming threat. Instead, they are happy to allow management to drift along, making marginal improvements that are woefully inadequate to keep pace with the emerging reality. After the path forward has been articulated, the board must play an active role, ratifying and disseminating the results of the catalytic-governance process, and then ensuring its implementation by monitoring the results. This step is not a simple, once-and-for-all end point; it is itself a process of action learning.

I have not given up trying to transform companies or industries or encouraging them to transform themselves. But I am also aware of the scale of the challenge and the need for a more concerted effort to develop and refine processes that encourage transformation. George Bernard Shaw's comment, mentioned earlier in chapter 4, neatly summed up the challenge: "Progress is impossible without change, and those who cannot change their minds cannot change anything."[14]

The purpose of step 2 (engagement and dialogue) and step 3 (exploring alternative perspectives and future scenarios) of the catalytic-governance process is to open participants' minds to the brutal realities of disruptive change. Only through dialogue with a diverse group of stakeholders can directors hope to gain a proper understanding of the threats and opportunities. Likewise, a group of individuals can create a shared vision only by working together to craft scenarios – in other words, plausible alternative stories about the future – and then rolling up their sleeves and putting the chosen strategy into practice. Such actions are the foundation for true transformational change.

CHAPTER EIGHT

The Information Age Changes Everything

The information revolution has been with us for almost half a century. Spurred by advances in computing and communications technology, we are now deep into an upheaval as earthshaking as the one following the invention of the printing press. The explosion of information and communications technology is just the latest in a series of advances that have transformed the global economy. Each wave has been driven by a new set of general-purpose technologies and new institutions. As they have swept through society, these waves have done more than just wash up new technologies and industries; each one has transformed the whole structure of the economy and many of society's fundamental assumptions and institutions.[1]

The Fourth Information Revolution

Like the first industrial revolution's steam-powered factories, the second industrial revolution's application of science to mass production and manufacturing, and the third's start into digitization, the fourth industrial revolution's technologies, such as artificial intelligence, genome editing, augmented reality, robotics, and 3-D printing, are rapidly changing the way we create, exchange, and distribute value. As was the case in earlier centuries, the current era will profoundly transform institutions, industries, and individuals.

More important, according to Klaus Schwab, founder of the World Economic Forum, this revolution will be guided by the choices that people make today: the world in fifty or a hundred years from now will owe much of its character to how we think about, invest in, and deploy these powerful new technologies.[2]

The digital era has unfolded at a dizzying pace, and its impact has been breathtaking. The Internet, used by a minuscule 0.45 per cent of the world's population in 1994, now reaches almost 60 per cent or 4.4 billion people – with thousands more coming online every day.[3] Mobile Internet access is exploding even faster, from zero in 2007 to more than 1 billion unique users in 2012 and an estimated 5.2 billion in January 2020.[4] The number of mobile Internet users surpassed desktop computer users in late 2016. According to Peter Diamandis, chairman of Singularity University, the pace of change is about to get even faster.[5]

Sometime around 2010 we encountered the fourth wave of general-purpose technologies (often referred to as the fourth industrial revolution) that blur the lines between the physical, digital, and biological spheres, collectively referred to as cyber-physical systems. Its progeny has included entirely new areas of human enterprise, such as robotics, artificial intelligence, nanotechnology, quantum computing, biotechnology, the Internet of Things, advanced wireless technologies, 3D printing, and driverless vehicles. These new technologies are disrupting almost every industry around the world. And the breadth and depth of these changes herald the transformation of entire systems of production, management, and governance.

As if all this is not enough, we are also, according to management guru Peter Drucker[6] and historian Niall Ferguson,[7] in the throes of a fourth information revolution. The first was the invention of writing, which started five or six thousand years ago in Mesopotamia, then – independently but several thousand years later – emerged in China and, some fifteen hundred years after that, among the Maya in central America. The second information revolution was triggered by the invention of the written book, first in China, perhaps as early as 1300 BCE, and then eight hundred years later, in Greece. The third revolution was sparked by Johannes Gutenberg's invention of the printing press and movable type in the mid-fifteenth century.

The impact of the printing press was at least as great as that of the revolution we are now living through. In Gutenberg's time, quite an efficient infrastructure was already in place for disseminating information. Thousands of highly skilled monks labored in their monasteries from dawn to dusk, six days a week, copying books by hand. But by 1500, the monks had been replaced by the first print-ers, a group of no more than a thousand lay craftsmen spread across Europe. A team of twenty could print at least five million pages a year, binding them into 25,000 books ready for sale. Their output amounted to 250,000 pages per craftsman, a far cry from the roughly 1,200 pages that each hard-working monk could produce just fifty years earlier.

Printing's greatest impact was on the church, the core of pre-Gutenberg Europe. Printing made the Protestant Reformation pos-sible. Its predecessors, the reformations of John Wycliffe in England (1330–1384) and of Jan Hus in Bohemia (1372–1415), had met with an equally enthusiastic popular response. But those revolts could not travel farther or faster than the spoken word and could thus be easily localized and suppressed. This was not the case when Luther, on 31 October 1517, nailed his ninety-five theses on a church door in an obscure German town. He had intended only to spark a traditional theological debate within the church; but, without his consent, the treatises were quickly printed and distributed all over Germany, and then across Europe. These printed leaflets ignited the firestorm that turned into the Reformation. Such shifts in society are hard to measure. But the impact on government, education, culture – let alone religion – of the printing revolution was as shattering as that of the twenty-first century's information revolution.

Even so, the revolution we are living through now is different from those that have gone before, not least because information is fundamentally different from physical assets.[8] For example,

- Information is *expandable*: It expands as it is used.
- Information is *not resource hungry*: Producing and distributing information requires very little in the way of energy and other physical or biological resources.

- Information is *substitutable*: It can and increasingly does replace capital, labor, and physical materials.
- Information is *transportable*: It moves at close to the speed of light.
- Information is *diffusive*: Information wants to be free; it leaks universally, pervasively, and continuously. Monopolizing information is almost a contradiction in terms.
- Information is *sharable*: If I sell you my automobile, you have it and I don't. But if I sell you an idea or give you a fact, we both have it, and others will likely soon have it too.

These attributes mean that we need to rethink many concepts we have taken for granted up to now. New technologies such as the personal computer, the Internet, downloadable software (apps), mobile smart devices, cloud computing, and social networks have spawned new industries and transformed services. They have changed the way we engage in manufacturing and farming, leading to huge improvements in productivity and turning national financial markets into global ones. It is no exaggeration to say that the information revolution has left nothing and nobody untouched. A new set of corporate giants has emerged, led by Apple, Google, Amazon, Facebook, Netflix, Alibaba, and Tencent, with many smaller companies nipping at their heels. These pioneers have nurtured new business models and countless possibilities for change.

And yet, the revolution has barely begun. We have still to feel the full impact of the next wave of technology – artificial intelligence, quantum computing, the Internet of Things, 3D printing, robots, and more. Admittedly, such fundamental change comes at a cost, undermining previously sturdy business models and altering the structure and economics of entire industries. Many businesses are no longer able to keep their heads above water, and workers without the skills to adapt find themselves in a downward spiral, raising tensions between "winners" and "losers," as recent political developments in the United States and Europe have vividly shown.

Like the printing press, electricity, and the steam engine in past centuries, the Internet – especially the mobile Internet – is a radical innovation (GPT) that is disrupting not only individual firms and industries but entire economies. As noted in chapter 2, e-commerce has already revolutionized the music, movie, newspaper, book publishing, and travel industries and is starting to disrupt other service sectors around the world, including retail, healthcare, education, and financial services.

Economic Transformation

Central to the digital transformation is a shift in the economy toward intangibles. In their 2018 book, tellingly titled *Capitalism without Capital*, Jonathan Haskel and Stian Westlake report that businesses in developed countries increasingly invest more in intangible assets (10 to 13 per cent of GDP) than in tangible assets. The intangibles economy is driven by ideas, mostly proprietary ideas and information – in other words, intellectual property. For an indicator of the importance of ideas in today's economy, consider what has happened to companies comprising the Standard and Poor's (S&P) 500 Index. In 1975, one-sixth of the S&P 500 represented the value of intangibles; today that figure is five-sixths.[9] The market value of Apple, Amazon, Alphabet, Microsoft, and Facebook is about US$4.8 trillion, with their tangible assets amounting to about 5 per cent (US$225 billion) of that figure.[10] Intangibles and intellectual property (IP) are not the same thing – intangibles also comprise, for example, goodwill and brand recognition. But the magnitude of the shift is telling as an indicator of the relative decline in the value of physical assets and the rise of technological advancements and intangibles.

The unusual economic characteristics of intangibles mean that their rise is more than a trivial change in the nature of investment. Haskel and Westlake argue that there are two big differences with intangible assets. First, most accounting conventions ignore them, which means we are trying to measure capitalism without counting all the capital. Second, the basic economic properties of intangibles make an intangible-rich (information) economy behave differently from a tangible-rich (industrial) one. It is marked by high upfront costs and very low reproduction costs. It conveys a great advantage to first movers, particularly if the technology becomes a global industry standard. It is often relatively easy for other businesses to take advantage of intangible investments made by others, although much of this cost can be offset by synergies to be gained from combining ideas with others.

Rohinton Medhora, president of the Centre for International Governance Innovation, talks about the need to rethink government policy in a digital world. "Robotics and artificial intelligence are pillars of the intangibles economy. Even if predictions of massive job losses from the introduction of robotics and AI are not borne out, this much is clear: career trajectories and the nature of work are being transformed. Career changes are likely to become more frequent. Skills upgrading will become more important, and multi-year, post-high school education programs will be less the norm, more likely to be replaced or complemented by lifelong learning opportunities. The traditional firm-employee relationship may even devolve into a series of simultaneous or sequential contractual relationships between workers and employers, or between workers."[11]

Although it's hard to pin down specific scenarios, two outcomes of the information revolution are already obvious. First, wealth creation will be driven by proprietary intellectual property. Second, this knowledge will be generated within only a few countries and by a very small number of individuals and firms. As a result, the income and wealth gap will surely worsen before it improves, if it ever does.

The implications for society are huge. The full impact of these new technologies – on businesses, jobs, education, health care, democracy, and, of course, corporate governance – has yet to become apparent. But one thing is clear: most companies will have to learn how to transform themselves if they are to remain relevant. And as mentioned earlier, successful corporate transformations, except for a few still managed by their founders, to date are almost nonexistent. Without more effective governance, many existing companies will fail, and new enterprises will struggle to keep up with the pace of change.

A Global Information Society Is Different

An "information society" is not simply a society that uses computing and deep learning or other AI technology. Rather, it is a completely new social, economic, and political order. While the term "information society" may conjure up images of specific technologies central to its emergence, its main legacy is the ever-closer connections between individuals, businesses, and governments, both within and across national boundaries. An increasingly interconnected society dissolves familiar boundaries. But boundaries are fundamental to identity, to organization, to culture, and to governance. Governance becomes a continual challenge of recognizing how those boundaries are shifting and developing more effective ways to work across them.

We have seen this dynamic play out over the past few decades. Enormous advances in information processing and telecommunications have given rise to the mobile Internet, social networking, cloud computing, smart devices, and an explosion in e-commerce. More recently, advances in neural networks have brought artificial intelligence to the cusp of transforming many more activities. The structure of work is changing as the economy becomes more globalized and more knowledge-based. The media – in the form of both traditional media and social media – have a vastly expanded reach. Much of the population has gained greater access to education, information, and the ability to organize, giving rise to an unfamiliar group of players, such as citizen groups that self-organize using social media in the hope of asserting a role in governance. And we have a much richer infrastructure of public and private organizations, reinforced by greater collaboration and debate.

As boundaries blur and change, and as basic conceptual distinctions need to be rethought, we are exploring a territory for which there is no reliable map. We usually describe our inability to make sense of ever greater volumes of unfamiliar information in terms of information overload. Instead, the problem may be that our existing frameworks and methods of interpretation – our existing mental maps – are inadequate to translate the wealth of data and information into meaningful knowledge. Redrawing our mental maps is a key to effective governance.

Peter Drucker drew a distinction between data, information, and knowledge, a distinction that is relevant to corporate governance. *Data*, he says, are like unrefined ore, made up of undifferentiated facts without context. *Information* is more like refined ore, in other words, data that are organized but that we have not yet internalized.[12] It consists, for example, of the newspapers we have not yet read, or the course of study we have yet to take. At the top of the scale is *knowledge*, the information we have internalized and integrated into our own intellectual frameworks. This distinction suggests that, in an information society, the task of effective governance is to initiate the process of translating data and information into knowledge: interpreting the data, giving them meaning, and so turning them into a useful basis for action.[13]

In the new information society, everything seems connected to everything else. But the enormous volume of information now available also carries the threat of greater overload, filtering, and denial of facts. It compresses both time and space, intensifying turbulence and unpredictability.

These changes have powerful implications for governance.

- The move towards a no-boundaries economy has created interconnected stock exchanges, borderless capital markets, global supply chains, and a push for businesses to operate on a regional or even international scale. More and more issues – including trade, the environment, and human rights – must be handled by networks and groups that transcend national and corporate boundaries.
- At the same time, we are seeing a trend towards atomization, democratization, and fragmentation. As regionalism grows and states fragment, subnational governments are becoming more powerful. Every nation and organization is having to take more voices into account as more groups assert a role in the issues that interest them.
- We are shifting away from a hierarchical, command-and-control model of organization. Governments and companies are

downsizing in many parts of the world, stripping away middle management, and contracting out or privatizing work. Increasingly, they rely on networks, task forces, and other flexible, decentralized, "client-centered" ways of doing their work.

- Leaner, less centralized organizations rely ever more heavily on people with specialized skills. Both public- and private-sector organizations depend on well-qualified staff who can manage large amounts of information, establish effective working relationships within and outside the organization, make independent judgments, and innovate. Traditional hierarchical governance was not designed to deal with independent workers. The burgeoning flow of information makes secrecy ever more elusive. Information runs through so many channels and access is so widespread that leaks have become almost the norm. This is a serious concern for governance systems that rely on a certain degree of confidentiality.
- We are also witnessing a fundamental restructuring of long-standing categories. Historical boundaries – between industries, between public and private sectors, and even between states – are blurring. As these entities search for new relationships and alliances, basic conceptual distinctions are being called into question.

In this complex, interconnected, and rapidly changing world, where boundaries are rapidly shifting, the very nature of leadership and governance must also transform. The likely impact of the information age on our systems of governance was articulated thirty-five years ago, in a prescient work by Harlan Cleveland. His insights, formulated well before the mass introduction of the Internet, are worth quoting at length:

Knowledge is power ... So the wider the spread of knowledge, the more power gets diffused. For the most part individuals and corporations and governments don't have a choice about this; it is the ineluctable consequence of creating – through education – societies with millions of knowledgeable people. More and more work gets done by horizontal process – or it doesn't get done. More and more decisions are made with wider and wider consultation – or they don't "stick." A revolution in the technology of organization – the twilight of hierarchy – is already well under way.

In the old days when only a few people were well educated and "in the know," leadership of the uninformed was likely to be organized in vertical structures of command and control. Leadership of the informed is different: it results in the necessary action only if exercised mainly by persuasion, bringing into consultation those who are going to have to do something to make the decision a decision. *In an information rich polity, the very definition of control changes. Very large numbers of people empowered by knowledge assert the right or feel the obligation to "make policy."* (Emphasis added.)[14]

Cleveland describes a deep-rooted cultural shift that has since been amplified and accelerated by technological change. As information is distributed ever more broadly, the very definition of control – of governance – must change to become more inclusive. Without wider dialogue, companies will continue opting for strategies that are ineffective and ill-suited to the demands of the age.

Powerful New Kids on the Block

The folks at Silicon Valley's Singularity University believe that the lifespan of an S&P 500 company, estimated at an average of fifteen years in 2014 by Yale University's Richard Foster, will shrink even further in years to come. The biggest corporations will find themselves competing with and then annihilated in short order by a new breed of enterprise that harnesses powerful new technologies such as collaborative software (known as groupware), data mining, synthetic biology, deep learning, and robotics.

The new powerhouses, known as exponential organizations, or ExOs for short, will have a disproportionately large impact – with an output at least ten times larger – compared to their peers.[15] But instead of employing armies of people or putting up huge plants, exponential organizations are built on information technologies that take what were once physical materials and convert them to the digital, on-demand world.

Two of the best-known ExOs are Airbnb and Uber. Founded in 2008, Airbnb currently has only about 1,300 employees but, as of late 2019, offered five million lodging options in 81,000 cities. It has few physical assets, yet it is estimated to be worth US$38 billion.[16] That's more than Hyatt Hotels, which has 45,000 employees working in 550 fancy properties around the world. Similarly, Uber, which transforms private cars into taxis, was valued at $82.4 billion at the time of its May 2019 public offering. Again, it has virtually no physical assets and a tiny full-time workforce.

The digital transformation is taking place wherever you look: in 2012, 93 per cent of US commercial transactions were already digital. Nikon and Canon have seen their clunky cameras, typically with an array of dials, buttons, and clip-on lenses, supplanted in short order by far simpler smartphone camera apps. Street maps and atlases have been replaced by GPS devices, which themselves are being replaced by smartphone sensors. Libraries of books and music are being turned into phone and e-reader apps. Similarly, retail stores in China are being forced out of business by the e-commerce tech giant Alibaba. Universities are being threatened by MOOCs (massive open online courses) such as edX and Coursera. Tesla S is as much a computer on wheels as it is a car. The list goes on …

Singularity's research into the one hundred fastest growing startups worldwide identified common traits among all ExOs. By definition they all think big. They aspire to capture the imagination of everyone around them with their aggressive sense of purpose. Ideally, the company's massive transformative purpose (MTP) is so inspirational that a community forms around the ExO and spontaneously begins operating on its own, ultimately creating a new culture. For example, Google's MTP is to "organize the world's information." The cultural shift inspired by the MTP has secondary effects. It moves the focal point of the company from internal politics to external impact, underlining the necessity for a modern enterprise to constantly look outward – not least so that it can spot looming technological, competitive, or regulatory threats.

In addition to their transformative purpose, ExOs draw on ten valuable assets – five external and five internal – to drive their impressive growth. The five external attributes – staff on demand, community and crowd, algorithms, leveraged (not owned) assets, and engagement – spur growth, creativity, and uncertainty. Using workers outside the base organization is key to creating and running a successful ExO. Building a community around an ExO means using the MTP to attract and engage early members, nurturing the community, and then creating a platform to automate peer-to-peer engagement. The crowd – those outside the core community – can be tapped to harness creativity and even funding in the form of crowdfunding. Algorithms – both machine learning and artificial intelligence – are being used to automate pretty much everything. By using information rather than tangible assets, such as bedrooms for Airbnb or automobiles for Uber, ExOs can gain access to physical assets anytime and anywhere, without having to possess the assets. Engagement with customers consists of digital reputation systems, games, and incentive prizes, providing the opportunity for virtuous, positive feedback loops – which in turn spurs faster growth thanks to more innovative ideas, and customer and community loyalty.

The five internal mechanisms – interfaces, dashboards, experimentation, autonomy, and social technologies – focus on order, control, and stability. ExOs expand beyond normal corporate boundaries by using outside people, assets, and platforms to achieve a level of agility and learning unfamiliar to pre–information-age businesses. Interfaces are algorithms and automated workflows that route information generated by the five externalities to the right people at the right time within an organization. Often, these processes start out manually but then gradually become automated, enabling the ExO to grow exponentially. Given the huge amount of data from customers and employees that is now available, ExOs need a way to measure and manage themselves; hence, a real-time, adaptable dashboard with all essential company and employee metrics, accessible to everyone in the organization. This fund of data answers two questions: Where do I want to go? How will I know I'm getting there?

Experimentation is a key part of the process, testing assumptions and constantly improving them. In today's fast-changing world, ExOs believe that constant experimentation and process improvement are the only ways to reduce risk. Rather than managing through organizational structure, reporting lines, job descriptions, and regular meetings, as most companies are accustomed to doing, ExOs manage through self-organizing, in the form of multi-disciplinary teams that operate with decentralized authority. Finally, ExOs use social technology[17] to reduce the distance between obtaining and processing information and decision making.

Leadership guru Edgar Schein believes that it is possible for founders to create a culture that, by its very nature, is learning-oriented, adaptive, and flexible.[18] However, a learning culture assumes that participants will be proactive problem solvers and learners. They must believe that they can, at least to some degree, manage, the environment around them and the future. They must be transparent in their communications and search for the truth through inquiry and dialogue. They must be committed to cultural diversity and rigorous planning.

Not every ExO has all these attributes, but most have many of them. Because they use real-time and not historical information to arrive at decisions, ratifications by the board of directors after the fact are meaningless. Governing these ExOs requires a new approach, one that shifts from hierarchy to networks, and from processes to principles. Replacing review processes with a core set of principles based on sound assumptions that are constantly tested empowers distributed, real-time decision making. The directors should be able to let go without losing control, while still being able to monitor the company's adherence to the principles.

Lessons for Governance

As the ever-astute Peter Drucker observed in 1999,

One thing is certain for developed countries – and probably for the entire world. We face long years of profound changes. The changes are not primarily economic changes. They are not even primarily techno-logical changes. They are changes in demographics, in politics, in soci-ety, in philosophy, and above all, in world-view. Economic theory and economic policy are unlikely to be effective in such a period. And there is no social theory for such a period either. Only when this period is over, decades later, are theories likely to be developed to explain what has happened.[19]

This reality has significant implications for corporate governance. No longer can directors ignore nonshareholder stakeholders. One hallmark of an information society is that employees, customers, suppliers, regulators, investors, and activists are able to build closer links with one another than ever before. We need more networked forms of management and governance to replace the shackles of hierarchy.

My goal in this book is to highlight not only how fast-moving information technology and the accompanying changes in society are disrupting business, but also that the vast majority of direc-tors and managers are failing to recognize the far-reaching impact of these changes. Even those that appreciate the enormity of the shift seem frozen in their tracks, unwilling or unable to equip their companies with the tools needed to adapt to the challenges of a new era.

In chapter 7, I outlined a collaborative process that enables busi-ness leaders to monitor disruptive change and catalyze a process to deal with it. Unfortunately, most North American and British com-panies are not well-placed to put this process into practice. For now, their directors and senior managers remain fixated on short-term performance designed to push up the share price – and their own compensation. Success in the information age will mean paying more attention to the longer term, recognizing that the earth beneath them is constantly shifting and that new governance processes are needed.

A fresh mindset will mean sharing responsibility for govern-ing with all stakeholders and recognizing that corporations exist to serve the communities in which they operate. The US

Business Roundtable took a big step in that direction in August 2019 with the announcement by 181 member CEOs that they were now committed to leading their companies for the benefit of all stakeholders – not just shareholders, but also customers, employees, suppliers, and communities. This was the first time the Roundtable had updated its governing principles since 1997 when it codified a singular dedication to maximize shareholder value. If the CEOs follow through with this expanded view of their responsibilities, it would mean a sea change for American capitalism.

The new infotech companies do not look anything like the hierarchical vertically integrated companies of the industrial age. The three largest US carmakers in 1990 – General Motors, Ford, and Chrysler – had a combined market value of $36 billion with 1.2 million employees.[20] In 2017, Silicon Valley's three largest companies – Apple, Alphabet (Google), and Microsoft – were valued at over $2.5 trillion but had just 252,000 employees. These days, the most successful companies operate with very few assets (including employees), instead relying heavily on partnerships with other companies, independent contractors, and customers. Given this structure and the expanded boundaries of a "firm," effective governance now means working with many more stakeholders – suppliers, customers, users, investors, policy makers, regulators, and nongovernment organizations.

The shift in processes and priorities is clear from the turmoil that has recently engulfed Facebook. Without well-defined regulatory boundaries, the company powered forward with a single-minded goal: to create as much wealth as possible for Mark Zuckerberg and other shareholders. It did not pay nearly enough attention to the mounting concerns of more than two billion users about who had access to their information and how it was being used. When the Cambridge Analytica scandal broke in January 2017, Facebook was caught flatfooted. It took three days (a lifetime in the information age) for Zuckerberg to give a less than satisfactory response. Months later, Facebook was still struggling to quell a torrent of criticism.

Regulators are finally starting to recognize the problem, even if they have yet to deal with it effectively. Privacy laws are being tightened and penalties stiffened. The lesson is that disruptive change is driven not only by technology but also by evolving social attitudes, which are often more difficult to perceive until they burst out into the open, as happened with the #MeToo movement in 2018. More about this in the next chapter.

CHAPTER NINE

A New Governance Model

As noted in the previous chapter, the US Business Roundtable took the unprecedented step in August 2019 of redefining the purpose of a corporation to serve all Americans, not just investors:

> While each of our individual companies serves its own corporate purpose, we share a fundamental commitment to all of our stakeholders. We commit to:
>
> - Delivering value to our customers. We will further the tradition of American companies leading the way in meeting or exceeding customer expectations.
> - Investing in our employees. This starts with compensating them fairly and providing important benefits. It also includes supporting them through training and education that help develop new skills for a rapidly changing world. We foster diversity and inclusion, dignity and respect.
> - Dealing fairly and ethically with our suppliers. We are dedicated to serving as good partners to the other companies, large and small, that help us meet our missions.
> - Supporting the communities in which we work. We respect the people in our communities and protect the environment by embracing sustainable practices across our businesses.

- Generating long-term value for shareholders, who provide the capital that allows companies to invest, grow and innovate. We are committed to transparency and effective engagement with shareholders.

Each of our stakeholders is essential. We commit to deliver value to all of them, for the future success of our companies, our communities and our country.[1]

This new purpose is a step in the right direction. It means that directors must now focus on creating longer-term value for all stakeholders.

Effective governance is essential to the future of capitalist society, and this has never been truer than now. To put it succinctly, engagement with a network of diverse stakeholders and learning are the cornerstones of governance in the information age. The information necessary for dialogue and decision making must be available and transparent. Directors must invest the time and resources necessary to develop a shared mental map, mutual understanding, and trust. Without this foundation, it will be impossible to build the mindset, behaviors, and processes necessary to govern the fast-growing organizations spawned by the information age.

Yet, as I have tried to make clear, existing standards of corporate governance come nowhere close to meeting these conditions.

Lessons from the Past

Although the information age is very different from the industrial age, the past holds several relevant lessons for the future. To recap the points made in earlier chapters:

1 The board is responsible for the overall stewardship of the corporation and, as such, its duties must include:

   - adoption of a corporate strategy;
   - succession planning, including appointing, training, and monitoring senior management;

- a communication program;
- maintaining the integrity of the corporation's internal control and management systems.

Sir John Harvey-Jones, one of Britain's most respected business leaders of the twentieth century, summed it up well: "The role of the board is to take the company purposefully into the future."

2 People see what they choose to see, rather than what is actually happening. To ensure the corporation is not blind-sided, directors and managers must learn to recognize and be prepared to confront reality. Tools such as searching for anomalies, scenarios, and dialogue can be helpful.

3 Organizations learn only through individuals who learn and share. Individual learning does not guarantee organizational learning. But without it no organizational learning occurs.

4 Changing a company's culture is not easy. Once the founders who established the culture have moved on, change is only likely as a result of a life-threatening event. In the rapidly changing information age, only an adaptable culture is likely to be a lasting one.

5 Judicious allocation of resources – human, intellectual, physical, financial, and social capital – is a critical component of governance. But the allocation of resources is not a one-time exercise. Rather, as the environment shifts, resources must be reallocated and business models tweaked to ensure continuing relevance.

6 Exiting a business, whether through sale, joint venture, or closure, is not only a viable strategy but often a necessary and attractive one. The resources needed for new ventures must be freed from the old business, if the company is to survive.

7 Resources, including access to information and the time and skills to analyze it, are essential for directors to make resource-allocation decisions. These resources can be provided by a corporate center.

8 Activist investors play an important role. When the directors are not doing their job – in other words, are not taking the

corporation purposefully into the future – then activist investors often step in to salvage as much value as they can. Private-
equity and venture-capital investors have much more at stake
than the typical director and are thus more inclined to do
whatever it takes to set the business on the right track. However, these investors have relatively short time frames (five
to seven years generally), which is much less than the time
required for most business transformations.

9 It is almost impossible to transform an existing business. The
only examples I can find are situations where the founders
have seen the writing on the wall and overhauled the business model, or where owners have sold a wilting business and
invested the proceeds in an entirely new enterprise. Most of
these transformations have taken decades to complete.

10 Successful corporations in the information age look and act
very differently from the industrial behemoths of the past.
They are, by design, learning organizations, prepared to innovate and experiment. Customers, employees, suppliers, and
communities are more connected and empowered. Progress is
monitored and decisions are made in real time with a higher
degree of transparency than in the past. Management and
governance are by necessity more networked.

These important lessons will need to be modified for the information age as the purpose of the corporation shifts from creating shareholder value to a much wider set of stakeholder goals, but one thing
is clear: only learning organizations are sustainable in an era of massive and rapid change.

Let's Put It Right

Company directors must prepare to face a series of governance
challenges if they are to have legitimacy in the twenty-first century.
While directors' duties remain much the same as they were fifty or
a hundred years ago, some far-reaching changes are needed in the
way they perform those duties. Just as the printing press enabled the

transition from individual, hand-lettered manuscripts to mass pub-
lications, so the mobile Internet is dramatically lowering the barriers
to the exchange of information.[2] Successful businesses in the information age will be marked by a small but engaged group of directors who never stop learning about the fast-changing world around
them, and never stop applying those lessons in the boardroom, in
the office, and on the shop floor.

Today's successful companies are not waiting for their auditors to
produce monthly, quarterly, or annual financial statements before
making decisions. Rather, they set out a bold vision of their future
and take the actions necessary to put it into practice through experimentation, collaboration, innovation, and community leadership. A
strategy is no longer a weighty document frozen in time but a continuous process of testing and learning. The same applies to innovation and leadership. Governance needs to be cast in the same mold,
constantly under review and always being tweaked to take account
of seismic shifts in the world around us.

Governance must shift from hierarchy to networks, and from
process to principles. To illustrate this shift, let us look at Wikipedia. Originally known as Nupedia, it was conceived as a free online
encyclopedia with content created by volunteers, but with a crucial
difference. The articles were evaluated in a multi-step review process. Nupedia produced a paltry twelve articles in its the first year.
But when the review process was replaced with a core set of principles that empowered distributed decision making, Wikipedia was
transformed into the behemoth it is today. Its founders were able to
let go without losing control. This same approach can be successful
for larger, more established businesses.[3]

The rules of engagement for the information age have yet to be
fully fleshed out. It is by no means clear who owns data about me
and what they should be allowed to do with the data. Shifts in culture and in society generally have a way of sneaking up on companies. New technology usually takes at least a decade before it catches
on, but the changes that it generates do not announce themselves.
Instead they creep into our lives until they are part of them, and
then there is no going back. Take sexual harassment, which has been

a topic of conversation for decades, but suddenly became a pressing public issue when the *New Yorker* and other media published accusations by dozens of women against the movie mogul Harvey Weinstein.

Likewise, Facebook scooped up hundreds of billions of users in the first years of its existence with scarcely a murmur about abuse of subscribers' data – until the Cambridge Analytica scandal broke in January 2017. Yet an improved model of corporate governance could have forestalled at least some of Facebook's problems.

Facebook, for Example

In January 2017, Mark Zuckerberg, founder and CEO of Facebook, was surrounded by controversy. The election of Donald Trump as the next president of the United States on 8 November 2016 had triggered a national storm of protests, and many put the blame at the door of fake news stories served up on Facebook's Trending Newsfeed. Facebook had launched the service in January 2014 to deliver stories that might be of interest to Facebook users, in addition to the automatic Newsfeed that told them what was going on in their social network. Individuals could select items that they were interested in, but an algorithm served up news items that might appeal based on past reading habits and those of their close friends. The argument against Facebook was that this process polarized public opinion, fueled prejudices, and encouraged the bitter partisan character of the election campaign. Some claimed that fake news, propagated through Newsfeed, supported the rise of anti-establishment sentiments among groups that felt left behind by the establishment elite.

Zuckerberg was unapologetic. On 10 November 2016 he commented, "Personally I think the idea that fake news on Facebook, which is a very small amount of the content, influenced the election in any way – I think it is a pretty crazy idea."[4] He argued that fake news stories were posted on both sides of the political spectrum. "Why would you think there would be fake news on one side and not the other?"[5] One technology critic wrote, "Confirmation bias doesn't begin to describe what Facebook offers partisans in both directions: a limitless, on-demand narrative fix, occasionally punctuated by articles grounded in actual world events, when those suit their preferences."[6]

On 17 March 2018, articles in the *New York Times* and Britain's *Observer* newspaper suggested that a political consultancy, Cambridge Analytica, had obtained detailed data about some fifty million Facebook users and shared this trove of information and analysis with third parties, including Trump's presidential campaign. According to the *Economist*, the result was a corporate crisis and a political reckoning. Between 16 March and 21 March, the firm's share price fell by 8.5 per cent, erasing $45 billion in market value.[7] Facebook was still the world's eighth most valuable publicly listed firm, but shareholders worried that politicians in Europe and America might impose onerous restrictions on data, suppressing growth.

Facebook's history proves how changes in society can surprise companies. If the company is not engaged in the community, it will have a hard time detecting how the ground is shifting beneath it. Senior executives, including Mark Zuckerberg, have been called to testify before the US Senate, while the Federal Trade Commission (FTC), the US government's main consumer watchdog, has launched an investigation into whether Facebook violated a deal to notify users about how their data are shared. In April 2018, the FTC ruled that Facebook had broken its word, and imposed a $5 billion fine. What's more, the company faces several complaints under new European Union data-protection regulations, and it has had to pay stiff fines in the United Kingdom, Italy, and the European Union for misusing private data.

As happens so often when a company is caught on the wrong foot, Facebook's response has been far too little, and far too late. It suspended around two hundred apps, pending investigation into whether they misused data. Facebook says it will in future conduct interviews, request information from the apps, and perform audits that may include on-site inspections. It also promised to double the number of employees dedicated to safety and security to more than twenty thousand by year-end 2019. Besides promising to comply with data protection rules, it is building a function for users to see what data have been collected and shared by websites, and allow users to delete data and restrict data collection in the future.

Despite these changes, Facebook remains badly out of sync with its users. A recent US survey showed that more than three-quarters of Americans were aware of the data-abuse scandal involving Cambridge Analytica. Some 94 per cent said they were worried about their data, and 57 per cent said that the scandal made them more concerned about their data privacy and security. More than two-thirds would like to see the US government put data-protection rules in place similar to those in Europe, which give individuals far more control over their information and oblige companies to handle their data more carefully.

The tougher approach to data collection and usage marks a significant disruptive change for Facebook and has exposed serious shortcomings in its governance systems. Had the company and its directors been more actively engaged in dialogue with a broad cross-section of stakeholders, especially the users who offer up their information, they would have been aware of rising concerns around data privacy and security. In the past, Facebook had been allowed to collect and use data to generate revenue, with few restrictions. But users are now making it clear that they are no longer prepared to accept such lax rules of engagement. Absent meaningful dialogue with its users, Facebook failed to fulfill their expectations, instead looking for quick and easy ways to patch up its existing – but clearly inadequate – business model. Clearly, Facebook and all other information-age companies need a new governance model to equip them for the times we are living in.

Zuckerberg announced Facebook's next pivot in March 2019 in the form of a "privacy-focused platform" around three of its key apps, WhatsApp, Instagram, and Messenger. The apps would be integrated, he said, and messages sent through them would be encrypted end-to-end, so that even Facebook could not read them. While it has not been made explicit, it is clear what the business model will be. Zuckerberg wants all manner of businesses to use its messaging networks to provide services and accept payments. Facebook will take a cut.[8] If the new strategy is successful it will transform a big part of Facebook's business.

Since Facebook is only fifteen years old and is still run by its founder, it is likely to have a much easier time putting a new business model in place than many other companies under more diffuse control. Studies by Bain & Company (*The Founder's Mentality*)[9] and Innosight, a consultancy founded by Clayton Christensen,[10] have found that transformations undertaken by founders have a much higher success rate than other attempts. One sterling example is Apple, transformed by Steve Jobs when he came back as CEO in 1997 and saved the company from near-bankruptcy and potential irrelevance by reinventing the PC with candy color iMacs, the digital music player, and the iPhone. Another is Netflix, which went from delivering mail-order DVDs to streaming video over the Internet. If Mark Zuckerberg's new strategy succeeds, banks and many other businesses that rely on private data will have much to worry about.

Significantly, many information-age technology companies, such as Facebook and Google, have issued dual-class shares, which give the founders super-charged voting rights.[11] Those privileged in this way maintain that it is important to protect their ability to make course-altering decisions. Research by the Rotman School's Centre for Governance Innovation supports this argument. Canada has allowed dual-class shares for more than sixty years,[12] and over the past forty years shares of companies controlled by a founding family, mostly through dual-class share structures, have outperformed those without controlling shareholders by 25 per cent.[13] While founders who wield voting control can put a company back on track in its early stages, this is unlikely to be an effective way to govern over the longer run because it is almost impossible to change the culture and business model of an organization once the founders move on.[14]

A New Model: From Hierarchy to Networks

The Facebook example highlights the urgent need for a new model of governance. A cozy group of like-minded – and often closed-minded – individuals is not equipped to steer a modern company, without constant input from a broad range of stakeholders. Constant dialogue with these parties is the foundation for governance in the information age. As discussed in the previous chapter, one of the keys to success for ExOs is the creation and nurturing of communities using social technologies.

Dialogue versus Debate

Dialogue is a powerful tool to build trust and create a shared language and framework. It enables a diverse group of individuals to come together and chart a common route forward.[15] Dialogue has an important advantage in that it includes an emotional dimension, something our conventional model of knowledge and learning tends to exclude. The dialogue model recognizes that strong feelings are bound to surface when fundamental values, interests, and cultural identity are at issue. We often rely on both facts and values when reaching our most important judgments, and dialogue takes account of this mix. Applied to corporate governance, it means that a well-functioning board of directors takes the emotional as well as the factual into account when making decisions.

Three features distinguish dialogue from everyday talking. For true dialogue to take place, participants must suspend their social status, treating one another as peers, listening with empathy, and allowing others to air long-held assumptions in a nonjudgmental way.

One way to understand the nature of dialogue is to contrast it with debate or advocacy, which is the way most board meetings function. While debate is a win/lose proposition, dialogue seeks to expand the terms of engagement and open new horizons (table 9.1). This is not to say that dialogue is good and debate bad. The two are based on different assumptions and have different purposes. The fundamental purpose of a debate is to win, while a dialogue aims to promote learning and understanding. You cannot "win" a dialogue, but it can open your mind to hitherto unthought-of possibilities.

Debate is an invaluable tool for clarifying differences and advancing a specific goal or agenda. It is often entertaining. Dialogue, however, excels at uncovering hidden assumptions, exploring unfamiliar

Table 9.1. Debate versus Dialogue

Debate/Advocacy	Dialogue
Assuming there is one right answer	Assuming others have pieces of the answer
About winning	About finding common ground
Listening for flaws	Listening to understand
Defending assumptions	Exploring assumptions
Seeking your outcome	Discovering fresh possibilities

alternatives, and mapping out common ground. Both are needed in a complex and rapidly changing world.

Unfortunately, dialogue has been largely underrated up to now in governance and decision making. The conventional approach tends to be straightforward: issues arise, key interests advocate for their preferred solution, and a decision is made. This may work well enough when the issues and the possible responses are well understood, and all participants share similar assumptions, background, and culture. But such uniformity is increasingly rare in the information age. As Facebook has found with data privacy, an additional step is needed when the issues and possible responses are unclear, and people with very different interests and priorities need to find common ground. That is where dialogue comes in (see figure 9.1).

Dialogue Precedes Decisions

One of this book's central themes is that dialogue is an essential precursor to decisions in the governance process. It is the only way to broaden perspectives, build trust, and find common ground. It does not replace debate, negotiation, or decision making. It precedes them, creating the mutual trust that is most likely to lead to a productive outcome.

Most important is that dialogue must be a continuing process that enables participants to construct shared norms and expectations. Within this framework, a diverse group of players can innovate and act on a series of initiatives to deal with disruptive change. Without it, effective leadership and governance will be impossible in the information age.

Figure 9.1. Dialogue and Decision Making: Adding the Missing Step

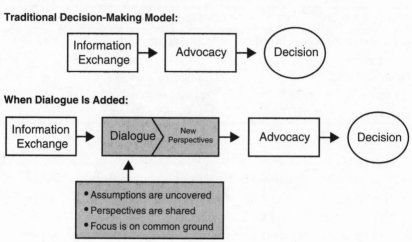

In the past, most systems of governance have been controlled by relatively small and homogeneous elites. Whatever agreement they reached was accepted and acted on by those around them – whether employees, suppliers, bureaucrats, or shareholders. Corporate governance still operates largely in this top-down manner as a form of "elite accommodation."

But, as I have sought to explain, the information age requires that we embrace a much broader range of stakeholders with diverse backgrounds and interests. The issues we now face cut across many boundaries – national, industry, organizational, regional, and more. What's more, the speed, complexity, and interconnectedness of change mean we can no longer separate planning and action in the traditional way.

Managing Uncertainty

Directors are also responsible for monitoring strategic risk, in other words, the risk that the wrong scenario occurs. Dialogue and scenario planning improve our capacity to manage uncertainty by showing us how much we *don't* know when it comes to disruptive change.

This can be disconcerting: many of us prefer to ignore uncertainty or erase it by simplifying our view of the world and our assumptions about how it works. However, these simplifications can betray us when we are trying to make weighty decisions – especially about unfamiliar issues or in times of crisis. Scenario planning requires directors to frame our concerns precisely and to focus on the issues that really matter, drawing a distinction between those that are relatively certain and likely to persist and those that are uncertain but likely to have a much greater impact.

Dialogue and scenario planning can help directors and senior executives consider plausible alternative futures and then find the common ground necessary to act on those forces about which they are reasonably certain, and to monitor those that are still uncertain, with a view to acting when the way forward becomes clearer. I believe this nimble approach to governance will be essential in navigating the digital age.

A Continuously Evolving Process

Board governance in the twenty-first century will be a learning process, involving multiple players, both within the company and beyond. Those in the lead will play a key role in framing and sustaining the dialogue with all players relevant to the company's future. This will be a continuous learning process, given that our ability to carry on conversations through social media is still in its infancy. To deal effectively with such a rapidly changing environment, boards need to develop new approaches that are more appropriate to shifts in the world around them.

From Process to Principles

We are just beginning to understand how to use real-time information as a management tool. But we can already sketch out major parts of the information system that enterprises need. Adaptable dashboards containing all essential company and employee data, accessible to everyone in the organization, are replacing quarterly and annual financial statements. These dashboards embed the principles underlying the company's vision and track key performance measures designed to ensure that actions are having the desired impact. This approach gives managers the autonomy they need to act quickly, and directors the information necessary to ensure that the company is on track

Directors and managers also need information about the key drivers of success (and failure) if they are to make wise decisions and monitor them properly. They need information about the company's cash-flow and liquidity to manage its financial resources. But they also need reliable information about the productivity and durability of the firm's other key assets – human, intellectual property, and physical capital.[16] They need information that will enable them to allocate all these resources efficiently in order to keep creating wealth.

Jon Lukomnik, executive director of the Investor Responsibility Research Center Institute and managing partner of Sinclair Capital, estimates that intangible assets now make up 84 per cent of the market value of S&P 500 companies, up from 17 per cent in 1975.[17] In other words, conventional financial statements disclose only 16 per cent of the value of a company, or its "book value" based on past transactions. As Warren Buffett observed in his 2019 letter to shareholders:

> Long-time readers of our annual reports will have spotted the different way in which I opened this letter. For nearly three decades, the initial paragraph featured the percentage change in Berkshire's per-share book value. It's now time to abandon that practice. The fact is that the annual change in Berkshire's book value – which makes its farewell appearance on page 2 – is a metric that has lost the relevance it once had.[18]

To remain relevant, accountants must develop a new model to explain wealth creation, one that includes intangibles such as human, intellectual, and social capital, the unique capabilities of the firm, the value of its data and network of relationships, and its contribution to society. The International Integrated Reporting Council (IIRC), a global coalition of regulators, investors, companies, the accounting profession, and NGOs, is promoting a dialogue on value creation as the next step in corporate reporting. Integrated reporting aims to measure everything of value to a broad a group of stakeholders. It aims to connect these elements in a way that makes their interdependencies clear. In doing so, it may represent the most significant change to the corporate reporting rulebook in years.

Even so, the accountants do not yet have a model for value creation. Mark Bonchek, founder of SHIFTthinking, has proposed one based on Einstein's famous formula of $E = MC^2$. Think of "E" as enterprise value. "M" is Mass, in other words, everything in an enterprise's universe. "C^2" is the ripple effect of connectivity and co-creation. In a traditional business, there is little connectivity or co-creation, so the enterprise value is equal to the "mass" of the company – its human resources, financial assets, intellectual property, and physical goods. By adding connections and co-creation, an enterprise multiplies the ability of these assets to create value.[19]

Conventional performance indicators tell us only about the business as it is currently constituted. They help devise tactics. But for broader, longer-term strategic decisions, companies need organized information about many more components of the world around them. Strategy must be based on information about markets, customers, and the world beyond – about relevant technology, worldwide finance, and the changing global economy. As discussed in chapter 3 and summarized by Peter Drucker,

> A serious cause of business failure is the common assumption that conditions – taxes, social legislation, market preferences, distribution channels, intellectual property rights, and many others – *must* be what we think they are or at least what we think they *should* be.[20]

Ideally, directors and managers should have access to information that challenges rather than confirms their assumptions and worldview. By actively participating in dialogue with numerous and different players through the company's social networks, directors are much more likely to become aware of shifts in the outside environment. This information should encourage them to ask probing questions, not just confirm their biases. And if decision making is to take place continuously, the directors must be tightly involved in the entire process.

These requirements reinforce the need for a chief external officer (or a "weaver"), as discussed in chapter 4. In today's fast-growing and complex businesses, the chief external officer would be responsible for managing the processes for outside stakeholders to engage in meaningful dialogue with directors and senior managers, and for providing real-time input to their decision-making processes. The chief external officer would work with the management team to weave together the information from all these sources and use it to buttress the company's decision-making processes.

Governance for the Information Age

Michael Jensen and many others are confident that the legally constituted corporate entity remains a viable option for rapidly growing enterprises with profitable investment opportunities that exceed the cash they generate internally.[21] But as Facebook's experience has shown, even new companies must be prepared for a major shift in direction if they are to survive and prosper. Fast-growing organizations that make a point of connecting with their communities and engaging relevant constituencies beyond are sure to have less trouble staying abreast of reality than their stodgy twentieth-century predecessors. Even so, an entirely new corporate model could emerge, looking more like a network of stakeholders joined together by their mutual interests.

Whatever the case, the principles of strategic governance remain the same. As discussed in chapter 2, the board will always be responsible for the long-term stewardship of the corporation. No matter what the model, the directors' top priorities should be:

- devising a long-term corporate strategy and being ready to change it as circumstances require;

- succession planning, which includes appointing, training, and monitoring senior management;
- effective communication, both internally and with the outside world, although this is much more likely to be accomplished using social networks;
- maintaining the integrity of internal control and management information systems.

In order to devise an effective strategy, the board must address two fundamental questions: What businesses should we be in? How should we organize them? It must also keep a constant lookout for new risks to the business that may result in having the "wrong scenario" occur. Answering these questions requires the board to proactively engage in a constant dialogue with stakeholders, and to monitor internal performance-measurement and management systems.

Many directors believe that the board's primary duty is to choose the right chief executive. As one long-time director recently told me, "If you do it well, your job will be a lot easier; if you don't do it well, you're in trouble."[22] But fulfilling this task does not absolve the board of its most critical responsibility: deciding what businesses the company should be in. In looking for the right CEO, it makes sense to know in advance where the company is headed, and what skills and capabilities are required to get there. The boss charged with disposing of a business has far less room to maneuver than one in a position to consolidate an industry or transform a company.

A sound governance system for the information age has five essential components:

- a compact board of directors (five to nine members) with decision-making authority and accountable to stakeholders for the long-term sustainability of the company. A diversity of perspectives is critical, as the more turbulent the environment, the more likely it is that a diverse board will be able to foresee and cope with unpleasant surprises;[23]

- a network of stakeholders, with effective processes and social technology to engage them. This body would be charged with promoting dialogue between and among directors, managers, employees, customers, suppliers, investors, regulators, policy makers, community representatives, and other stakeholder groups as issues arise;
- a chief external officer, reporting to the chair of the board and responsible for gathering and organizing external information and managing the processes to engage all stakeholders;
- a principles-based system of transparent performance indicators and internal controls aligned with the company's vision that gives employees the autonomy they need to make quick decisions;
- finally, a clearly articulated and measurable model of value creation to assess whether the company is on the right track.

The board's core role – to ensure that the actions taken are in the best long-term interest of the corporation – is indispensable to this process. Its fundamental responsibilities remain the same, but it needs to carry them out differently in the information age. Instead of simply reviewing and ratifying management's strategic plans, the board must take an active part in dialogue with all stakeholders, while being on the lookout for signals that something is not quite right. When it becomes clear that a problem is looming, the board must decide how to address it using the tools outlined above.

This is the time for catalytic governance. It involves leading transformative change that engages a wide range of stakeholders in dialogue and empowers them to envisage and enact a desired future. The board plays an important role by driving the process forward and monitoring its implementation.

The first step in catalytic governance, as shown in the chart on pages 116–17, is for the board to determine whether it is needed in the first place. Issues that are easy to resolve will not require a large investment of time and resources and can be addressed through traditional approaches. But catalytic governance is needed when both the issue and the possible responses are unclear, and when people with different beliefs, problem definitions, values, or traditions need to come together to find common ground.

In those circumstances, it is up to the board to frame the problem and the agenda, define the governance process to be followed and the range of stakeholders to be included, and set the boundaries for acceptable solutions. Above all, the directors need to be prepared to trust the process, and to place the onus on the stakeholders to deliver an acceptable outcome.

Let us use Facebook once again to illustrate how my proposed governance model would deal with that company's data-privacy challenges. First, effective stakeholder dialogue, especially with users who supply the data, would have made directors and managers aware of rising privacy and security concerns. Second, the directors would have begun to question the validity of Facebook's assumption that it could use the data collected to make money in any way it wanted. Using the catalytic governance process, the company would have engaged a diverse group of stakeholders to better understand its privacy and security issues and explore alternative approaches to address their concerns, while allowing Facebook to continue creating value for its shareholders. At a minimum, this process would have better prepared directors and managers to respond effectively when the crisis hit. Ideally, it would have positioned Facebook to lead the world in establishing the highest standards of privacy and security for personal data, in the process giving it an unassailable competitive advantage.

Once steps 2, 3, and 4 (see chart) of the process are complete, the board again has a pivotal role to play, first by ratifying and disseminating the results of the governance process, then by directing action on the emerging strategy, and finally by monitoring the results. This step 5 is not a simple, once-and-for-all end point; it is itself a learning process. The board retains the authority to withhold its approval and even to veto the outcome. However, given the degree of stakeholder engagement and investment in the process, any veto would require a clear explanation. Once an outcome is ratified, the directors have a duty to build widespread support for action beyond the stakeholders who have been directly involved up to that point.

Call to Action

Revamping our corporate governance system should be an urgent priority for anyone with an interest in seeing capitalism survive and thrive. Business has taken a heavy knock to its reputation over the past twenty years, and with good reason. All too often, corporate chieftains have been handsomely rewarded for failure. Short-sighted boards have steered once-proud companies onto the rocks, with devastating effects on workers, customers, suppliers, and local communities. Meantime, directors have chosen to look the other way as disruptive forces have buffeted the businesses for which they have supposedly been accountable. Without access to information about the brutal realities of the external environment, it is almost impossible for the board to consider plausible alternative scenarios to the one the company is currently living.

Much of the blame for this state of affairs belongs to antiquated and ineffective governance. Directors and managers have all too often failed not only to detect existential risks but to prepare their businesses for the changes needed to avert a full-blown crisis. Worse, the present system has actually encouraged such negligence through poorly designed compensation structures and inadequate accountability. An annual "offsite strategy" session with an agenda prepared by management does not fulfill the board's responsibility to ensure that the company has a sustainable corporate strategy – in other words, that the company is in the right business with the right business model and structure.

Without corrective action, the situation will only grow worse. The information age has stepped up both the pace and the intensity of change, underlining the need for structures that encourage corporate leaders to broaden their horizons, look beyond them, and listen to many more voices than most have in the past. But transformation takes time, as Thomson Corporation's experience shows. Building an entirely new enterprise can be a multi-year if not multi-decade journey.

Without a more inclusive governance system, many more companies will be forced to restructure, not on their own terms but by activist investors who see opportunities in repurposing the company's assets, or by ruthless managers hired by the board to eke out some value from whatever assets remain.

Governance in the information age must be an integrated process where the directors are continuously learning with the rest of organization. They must determine what path the company should follow, oversee its performance to ensure that the strategy is on track to produce the desired results, be on the lookout for changes in the environment that require a strategic response, and provide advice to senior management, if they ask for it.

As Dominic Barton and Mark Wiseman observed in their *Harvard Business Review* article:

> If directors keep their fiduciary duty to shareholders firmly in mind, big changes in the boardroom should follow. They would spend more time discussing disruptive innovations in the world beyond that could lead to new goods, services, markets and business models. They would ask what it takes to capture opportunities with big upside over the long term and, conversely, which operations no longer fit and should be discarded. They would spend less time talking about how to meet next quarter's earnings expectations, how to comply with regulations, and how to avoid lawsuits.[24]

Time is running out. If responsible business leaders fail to act, other, less scrupulous players will seize the initiative. Corporations will become even less accountable than they are now, raising the prospect of an even stronger backlash from newly assertive stakeholders – not to mention politicians spurred on by increasingly angry constituents. Public companies, if not capitalism itself, could be at risk.

Acknowledgments

This journey would not have been possible without the support of many colleagues (past and present), mentors, friends, and family members, only some of whom I can mention here. First and foremost, I would like to thank the four individuals to whom this book is dedicated – Jim Williams, Al Flood, Michael Jensen, and Steven Rosell. Sadly, Jim and Steve are no longer with us. Without these four men's influence throughout my career, this book would not have been written. As explained in the introduction, each has made a uniquely valuable impact in shaping my views on corporate governance.

The journey began at CIBC. My colleagues in the corporate center – John Hunkin, Holger Kluge, John Doran, Gerry Beasley, Derick Hayes, Don McLeash, and Peter Watkins – were instrumental in developing and implementing the corporate and business unit strategies outlined in chapter 1. I would especially like to thank one former colleague, who prefers not to be named, for reading chapter 1 to ensure that my memories are accurate (or at least aligned with his). The staff in the corporate strategy group – Sandra Stewart, Niki Root, Denise Ellis, Lisa Lunenburg, Michelle Moore, Leigh Merlo, Mark Richter, Darell Kletke, Heather Sparrow, and Terry Troy – did much of the work with the individual business units, analyzing and evolving their strategic thinking. Of course, none of our successes would have been possible without the dedication of thousands of CIBC employees who worked tirelessly to implement the many strategies; for them, it was exciting to be part of an innovative bank in an industry known for its stodginess.

For fifteen years I worked with Monitor Group (now Monitor Deloitte) to develop and implement competitive, organizational, and human strategy. Michael Wenban, Jonathan Goodman, Michael Jensen, Roger Martin, and Emma Barnes were tremendous colleagues and partners. Not only did they help shape my thinking on strategy and governance, but together we wrote and delivered a slew of strategy presentations to boards. I especially enjoyed Michael Wenban's long lunch conversations about the many failures of corporate governance.

I have also had the good fortune to work with five amazing individuals at various stages of my career. Geoff Beattie, former vice-chair of Thomson Corporation, president of Woodbridge, and a long-time director of General Electric, generously shared his thoughts on the role of owners and board members. He also arranged for me to interview John Tory and Ken Thomson about Thomson Corporation's transformation. Barbara Stymiest – former TSX Group CEO, RBC senior executive, and one of Canada's busiest corporate directors – reviewed this book (and my two previous ones). Mark Wiseman and David Denison, former CEOs of the CPP Investment Board, made me very aware of "governance arbitrage" and private equity's governance advantages. Dominic Barton, former McKinsey managing partner and now Canada's ambassador in China, was in the room when Al Flood chose to create a corporate center. Since then we have had many fascinating discussions on strategy and governance.

I would also like to thank three activist directors – John Vivash, Bill Waters, and Lawrence Bloomberg. They demonstrated that boards can make tough choices when confronted with the brutal reality. They also reaffirmed the importance of having a significant ownership stake when making those choices.

Much of my thinking about governance in the information age was tested by the governance working group of the Task Force for the Payments System Review. The task force recognized that in a rapidly changing environment, traditional hierarchical approaches to governance could not keep up. Instead, it recommended a stakeholder-engagement, principles-based approach overseen by a small, diverse group of stakeholders. Unfortunately for Canadians, the government appointed a traditional board of directors for Payments Canada, which has slowed our transition from paper payments to digital payments to a crawl. John Seely Brown, independent co-chair of the Deloitte Center for Edge Innovation, in his presentation to the payments task force, made the point that governance is the biggest unsolved problem of the information age, an observation that has motivated me for the past decade.

Over the past two years, I have worked closely with CPA Canada, especially Tashia Batstone, Gord Beal, and Gigi Dawes – on reimagining the accounting profession for the information age. A critical element of the accounting profession's future depends upon its ability to design and implement an effective governance model. I am grateful to them for clarifying the important role that accountants will continue to play in governance – both in measuring value creation in an intangibles economy and in providing real-time information for decision making.

The many boards that I have sat on over the past twenty-five years have helped to crystallize my views. Two stand out: the Canadian Institute for Advanced Research (CIFAR) and Sceptre Investment Counsel. Douglas Grant, Arthur Scace, and Ross Walker tutored me in public-company governance. Barbara Stymiest, David Dodge, Bruce Mitchell, Stephen Toope, and Richard Ivey have been exemplary chairs of CIFAR.

David Beatty and Matt Fullbrook of the David and Sharon Johnston Centre for Corporate Governance Innovation at the Rotman School of Management at the University of Toronto have provided invaluable assistance. For the past six years they have given me a place to work and provided many thoughtful insights. Their research into family-controlled businesses and focus on private-equity governance have helped to confirm the costs of ineffective traditional board governance of public companies.

Rohinton Medhora at the Centre for International Governance Innovation suggested I add more on the economics of the information age, an addition that greatly improved this book. Now that this project is complete, I am looking forward to working more closely with him and CIGI to operationalize inclusive governance.

Most importantly, I would like to thank those who contributed directly to the book. Luke Stacey, Alex Walker Turner, and Katya Belkina did most of the research on the various case studies. Krista Pawley recommended books and people for me to consult about the information age. She is also doing a tremendous job of raising my profile and marketing my books. Bernard Simon edited my many drafts. Without his help I would never have finished this book. Not only did he suggest a way for me to get started by telling my story about CIBC's fateful choice, but he also encouraged me whenever I ran out of energy for another round of revisions. Three anonymous reviewers gave us invaluable feedback and helped to improve the manuscript immeasurably. And last but not least, my editor, Jennifer DiDomenico at the University of Toronto Press, has been incredibly patient as one deadline after another slipped by. She has provided welcome guidance and encouragement and many helpful suggestions.

Finally, a special word of gratitude to those closest to me – my husband, Stephen Karam; son, Patrick Meredith-Karam; mother, Gloria Meredith; and dear friends Christine Croucher, Hanna Mayer, Gail Wdowiak, Hazel Copp, and Frances Michener. They all listened patiently as I bellyached about having to do yet another rewrite and gave me the fortitude to keep going. Thank goodness, it's now over!

Appendix A: Timeline for GE Post Trian Partners Presentation

12 June 2017
- Announcement that CEO Jeff Immelt would be replaced by GE Healthcare executive John Flannery on 1 August 2017. Immelt to retire as chairman of the board effective 31 December 2017.

2 October 2017
- Immelt retires as chairman of the board, Flannery elected chairman. Immelt also retires as director and chairman of Baker Hughes.

6 October 2017
- GE announces major changes to senior executive team amid significant cost-saving initiative. Vice-chairs Bett Comstock and John Rice and CFO Jeffrey Bornstein retire.

9 October 2017
- GE elects Ed Garden of Trian Partners to the board of directors. Trian Partners has a $1.6 billion stake in GE stock.

20 October 2017
- Earnings fall short of investor expectations. Company cuts its forecast for the year to $1.05–$1.10 from $1.60–$1.70.

13 November 2017
- Stock dividend cut in half from $0.24 per share to $0.12, because of a cash shortage.

7 December 2017
- GE announces plans to reduce its global headcount by twelve thousand positions in the power division.
- This is aligned with the company's goal of reducing structural costs by $3.5 billion in 2017 and 2018.

16 January 2018
- GE discloses $6.2 billion charge related to costs incurred more than a decade earlier by the Financial Services division. This triggers an investigation by the SEC over whether GE made overly aggressive assumptions to boost earnings.
- A comprehensive review and reserve testing for GE Capital's insurance business (North American Life and Health) results in additional statutory reserve contributions of $15 billion over seven years.

26 February 2018
- New board of directors slate of twelve includes three new directors, including H. Lawrence Culp, Jr.

21 May 2018
- GE spins off its railroad and locomotive business to Wabtec Corporation in a deal valued at $11 billion. GE will receive $2.9 billion cash, and GE shareholders will receive 50.1 per cent ownership interest in the combined entity.
- To raise cash, GE has promised to sell off about $20 billion worth of businesses including the iconic lightbulb division. The company signaled it was willing to break up the conglomerate.

19 June 2018
- GE, the last original member of the Dow Jones Industrial average, is dropped from the index.

26 June 2018
- GE announces plans to spin off its healthcare unit and separate its stake in oil services company Baker Hughes over the next two to three years.
- The company announces that it will be focusing on aviation, power, and renewable energy going forward.
- Lawrence Culp, Jr., former CEO of Danaher, becomes lead director.

20 July 2018
- GE announces a 30 per cent decline in second-quarter profits from the previous year, as a result of weakness in the Power Division.

1 October 2018
- Lawrence Culp, Jr., becomes chairman and CEO of GE. The board indicates that it is not satisfied with the pace of execution by previous CEO Flannery.
- GE announces it expects to take a $22 million goodwill impairment charge related to GE Power.

30 October 2018
- GE announces a 33 per cent decline in third-quarter earnings from the previous year and reduces the quarterly dividend from $0.12 per share to $0.01.
- GE announces it intends to reorganize GE Power, creating two business units: Unified Gas, including the gas products and service groups, and the remaining power assets.

12 November 2018
- GE shares close below $8 per share for the first time since March 2009.
- To reduce leverage the company is considering an IPO of the healthcare business, sale of the transportation business, and exit of the Baker Hughes oilfield-services business.

13 December 2018
- GE announces plans to establish an independent company focused on building a comprehensive Industrial Internet of Things software portfolio.

25 February 2019
- GE sells BioPharma business to Danaher for $21.4 billion.

2 April 2019
- GE completes sale of Current (a 2015 internal start-up designed to decrease energy use and increase operational productivity for commercial offices, retail stores, industrial facilities, and municipalities) to American Industrial Products.
- GE completes sale of Transportation Division to Wabetec Corporation.

Appendix B: Selected History of the Thomson Corporation

1934
- Roy Thomson acquires his first newspaper in Canada, *The Timmins Press*, Ontario.

1953
- Roy Thomson acquires his first newspaper in the United Kingdom, *The Scotsman*.

1957
- Successful bid for commercial television franchise for central Scotland, named Scottish Television.

1959
- Acquisition of the Kemsley Group, a UK publicly listed company, comprising national and regional newspapers, including *The Sunday Times*; merger of new acquisitions with Scottish Television and *The Scotsman* newspaper.

1961
- Thomson Publication (UK) formed to launch and acquire business and consumer magazines and book publishing companies.

1965
- Creation of Thomson Travel in the United Kingdom by acquisition of tour operating companies and Britannia Airways.

- Formation of Thomson Newspapers, Ltd., as a public company in Canada.

1967
- Acquisition of *The Times* of London and, with *The Sunday Times*, formation of Times Newspapers.

1971
- Thomson joins consortium to explore for oil and gas in the North Sea (UK).

1976
- Roy Thomson passes away and is succeeded as chairman by his son, Kenneth Thomson.

1977
- Final disposal of interest in Scottish Television.
- Thomson Newspapers' total daily circulation in the United States passes the one million mark.

1978
- Major expansion in specialized information and publishing launched in the United States with the acquisition of Wadsworth, a college textbook and professional book publisher.
- Financial restructuring of UK activities and formation of International Thomson Organisation Limited, with headquarters in Toronto and two main operating subsidiaries in the United Kingdom and the United States.

1980
- Thomson acquires Warren, Gorham & Lamont, a major information source for finance professionals.

1981
- Thomson sells *The Times* of London to News International, Ltd. (UK).
- Thomson acquires Litton (renamed Medical Economics) and Delmar, a publisher of career, technical, and vocational textbooks and course material.

1989
- Thomson Newspapers merges with International Thomson to form The Thomson Corporation.
- Thomson acquires Lawyers Co-operative Publishing Company.
- Thomson disposes of interests in North Sea oil in the United Kingdom.

1992
- Thomson acquires MicroMedex, a leading provider in the fields of healthcare, toxicology, and environmental health.
- Thomson acquires Institute for Scientific Information, a leading provider of information for researchers.
- Thomson acquires Course Technology, a worldwide leader in computing education for business and technology.

1994
- Thomson acquires Information Access Company, a US provider of broad-based reference and database services.
- Thomson acquires the Medstat Group, a US provider of healthcare-information databases and decision-support software.

1995
- Thomson divests interests in UK newspapers.
- Thomson acquires Peterson's, a leading provider of information.

1996
- Thomson acquires West Publishing, a leading US provider of legal information.

1998
- Thomson nets US$2 billion from sale of Thomson Travel.

1999
- Thomson acquires Editorial Aranzadi S.A., Spain's premier legal publisher.
- Thomson acquires Macmillan Library Reference USA, a group of publishers specializing in high-quality reference products for the library, secondary education, and college/university markets.

2000

- Thomson sells community newspaper assets in North America for approximately US$2.5 billion.
- Thomson acquires Greenhaven Press and Lucent Books, publishers of social issues and other nonfiction series for middle and high school students.
- Thomson acquires La Ley, a leading legal publisher in Argentina.
- Thomson acquires Primark, a leading provider of financial and economic information products and solutions to customers worldwide.
- Thomson acquires Carson Group, a financial-information-services firm focused on corporate strategic intelligence and investor relations solutions.
- Thomson acquires IOB, one of Brazil's leading regulatory publishers.
- Thomson acquires online business of Dialog, a leading worldwide provider of online-based information services.
- Thomson acquires Wave Technologies International, a provider of a flexible blend of self-study, classroom training, proactive mentoring, and testing.
- Thomson acquires Prometric, a global leader in computer-based testing and assessment services.
- Thomson acquires Physicians World, a full-service provider of medical education and communications programs for physicians and allied healthcare professionals.

2001

- Thomson acquires NewsEdge Corporation, a global provider of real-time news and information.
- Thomson acquires select higher education and corporate training businesses of Harcourt General.
- Thomson acquires FindLaw, the leader in free online legal information and services.
- *The Globe and Mail* becomes part of Bell Globemedia, a Canadian multimedia company, in which the Thomson Corporation holds a 20 per cent ownership position.

2002

- Thomson announces a $300-million-plus five-year deal with Merrill Lynch to develop and implement a new financial workstation.
- Thomson acquires *Current Drugs*, a global leader in the delivery of information solutions to the pharmaceutical and biotechnology industries.
- Thomson common share offering raises US$1 billion.
- Thomson begins trading on New York Stock Exchange under the symbol TOC.

2003

- Thomson sells print-based healthcare magazines.
- Thomson acquires Elite Information Systems, a leading provider of integrated practice and financial management applications for legal and professional services markets.
- Thomson sells its 20 per cent interest in Bell Globemedia Inc. for $279 million to the Woodbridge Company Limited.

2004

- Thomson acquires KnowledgeNet, a leader in live e-learning.
- Thomson acquires Capstar, a developer of learning and measurement solutions.
- Thomson acquires Information Holdings Inc., a provider of intellectual property and regulatory information for the scientific, legal, and corporate markets.
- Thomson sells Thomson Media group, comprising leading print-based information products, to Investcorp.
- Thomson acquires CCBN, a provider of web-based solutions for the investment community.
- Thomson sells DBM (Drake Beam Morin), which was acquired along with other Harcourt assets in 2001.

Notes

Preface

1 Jonathan Haskel and Stian Westlake, *Capitalism without Capital* (Princeton, NJ: Princeton University Press, 2018), 280.

1. CIBC: A Fork in the Road

1 These events were widely reported on by the Canadian media at that time. The sources provided were among several available.
2 Brenda Dalglish, "Turmoil at the Top," *Maclean's*, 7 January 1991. https://archive.macleans.ca/article/1991/1/7/turmoil-at-the-top.
3 Bloomberg, "CIBC Weighs Break with 100 Years of Tradition in Outside Search for CEO," *The Star*, 26 June 2014. https://www.thestar.com/business/2014/06/26/cibc_weighs_break_with_100_years_of_tradition_in_outside_search_for_ceo.html.
4 Steve Maich, "Fate's Favourite Fall Guy," *Maclean's*, 10 December 2004. https://archive.macleans.ca/article/2004/12/20/fates-favourite-fall-guy.
5 Brenda Dalglish, "Banking on Change," *Maclean's*, 2 November 1992. https://archive.macleans.ca/article/1992/11/2/banking-on-change.
6 Dalglish, "Turmoil at the Top."
7 CIBC, 1997 Annual Report, 15.

8   Funding Universe, "Canadian Imperial Bank of Commerce History."
    http://www.fundinguniverse.com/company-histories/canadian
    -imperial-bank-of-commerce-history/.

9   Mark S. Bonham, "Canadian Imperial Bank of Commerce (CIBC)."
    The Canadian Encyclopedia, 20 April 2006; last edited 14 January 2019.
    https://www.thecanadianencyclopedia.ca/en/article/canadian
    -imperial-bank-of-commerce.

10 Walter Stewart, *Too Big to Fail: Olympia and York: The Story behind the
    Headlines* (Washington, DC: Beard Books, 1993), 235.

11 Maich, "Fate's Favourite Fall Guy."

2. A Broken System

1   Williams Inference Global. (2018–2020). "Discovery Begins with the
    Awareness of an Anomaly." http://www.williamsinferenceglobal
    .com/what-we-do. Accessed on 8 June 2020.

2   Quotefancy. (nd). Bill Gates quotes. https://quotefancy.com
    /quote/775051/Bill-Gates-Banking-is-necessary-banks-are-not.
    Accessed on 8 June 2020.

3   Walter Isaacson, *Steve Jobs* (New York: Simon and Schuster, 2011), 565.

4   US Bureau of Labor Statistics, "Employment Trends in Newspaper
    Publishing and Other Media, 1990–2016," *TED: The Economics Daily*,
    2 June 2016. https://www.bls.gov/opub/ted/2016/employment
    -trends-in-newspaper-publishing-and-other-media-19 90-2016.htm.

5   Amy Watson, "Physical Album Shipments in the U.S. from 1999 to
    2019," *Statista*, 2 March 2020. https://www.statista.com/statistics
    /186772/album-shipments-in-the-us-music-industry-since-1999/.

6   "Sorry Banks, Millennials Hate You," *Fast Company*, 24 March 2016.
    https://www.fastcompany.com/3027197/sorry-banks-millennials
    -hate-you.

7   Charlie Rose, "Charlie Rose Talks to Cisco's John Chambers,"
    Bloomberg News, 19 April 2012. https://www.bloomberg.com/news
    /articles/2012-04-19/charlie-rose-talks-to-ciscos-john-chambers.
    Accessed on 8 June 2020.

8   Scott D. Anthony, S. Patrick Viguerie, Evan I. Schwartz, and John Van
    Landeghem, "2018 Corporate Longevity Forecast: Creative Destruction

Is Accelerating," *Innosight*, 2018. https://www.innosight.com/insight/creative-destruction/.

9 "Age of Disruption: Are Canadian Firms Prepared?" Deloitte, 2018. https://www.corpgov.deloitte.ca/en-ca/Documents/StrategyAndRisk/AgeOfDisruption_042015.pdf. Accessed on 8 June 2020.

10 Ibid.

11 Arie de Geus, *The Living Company: Habits for Survival in a Turbulent Business Environment* (Brighton, MA: Harvard Business School Press, 1997), 1.

12 Michael C. Jensen, "Eclipse of the Public Corporation," *Harvard Business Review*, September-October 1989, 62.

13 "The Endangered Public Company Briefing: The Big Engine That Couldn't," *The Economist*, 19 May 2012.

14 "A Plan for American Capitalism," *The Economist*, 26 October 2019.

15 Peter Drucker, *Management Challenges for the 21st Century* (New York: Harper-Collins, 1999), 74–80.

16 The Cadbury Report, "The Financial Aspects of Corporate Governance," December 1992. https://www.icaew.com/-/media/corporate/files/library/subjects/corporate-governance/financial-aspects-of-corporate-governance.ashx?la=en.

17 The author reviewed the top ten corporate governance books listed on Amazon. Although each of these books was several hundred pages in length, none of them contained more than a page or two about boards' discharging their responsibility for setting and reviewing corporate strategy or for monitoring strategic risk.

18 Thierry Dorval, *Governance of Publicly Listed Corporations* (Markham, ON: LexisNexis Canada Inc., 2005).

19 Michael E. Porter, "What Is Strategy?" *Harvard Business Review*, November-December 1996, 4.

20 A.G. Lafley and Roger L. Martin, *Playing to Win: How Strategy Really Works* (Boston: Harvard Business Review Press, 2013), 14.

21 Michael E. Porter, *Competitive Advantage: Creating and Sustaining Superior Performance* (New York: The Free Press, 1985), chapter 13.

22 https://www.brainyquote.com/quotes/mark_zuckerberg_453450.

23 Peter L. Bernstein, *Against the Gods: The Remarkable Story of Risk* (New York: Wiley, 1996), 337.

24 Michael C. Jensen, "The Modern Industrial Revolution, Exit and the Failure of Internal Control Systems," *The Journal of Finance*, XLVIII, 3 (July 1993), 850.

25 Ibid., 853.

26 Tellingly the name of his report was "Where Were the Directors?" https://thegrcbluebook.com/grc-articles/dey-report-on-corporate -governance.

27 Carol Hansell, *Corporate Governance* (Toronto: Thomson Carswell, 2003), 3.

28 Ibid., 49–50.

29 For an excellent discussion of the debate in the United States, see Lynn Stout, *The Shareholder Value Myth: How Putting Shareholders First Harms Investors, Corporations and the Public* (San Francisco: Berrett-Koehler Publishers, Inc., 2012).

30 Bob Tricker, *Corporate Governance: Principles, Policies and Practices*, 3rd ed. (Oxford: Oxford University Press, 2015), 224.

31 PricewaterhouseCoopers, "PwC's Annual Corporate Directors Survey 2018." https://www.pwc.es/es/publicaciones/consejos-y-buen -gobierno/pwc-annual-corporate-directors-survey-2018.pdf.

32 Dominic Barton and Mark Wiseman, "Where Boards Fall Short," *Harvard Business Review*, January-February 2015. https://hbr.org /2015/01/where-boards-fall-short.

33 McKinsey & Company, "A Time for Boards to Act," March 2018. https://www.mckinsey.com/business-functions/strategy-and -corporate-finance/our-insights/a-time-for-boards-to-act.

34 Barton and Wiseman, "Where Boards Fall Short."

35 Thomas S. Kuhn, *The Structure of Scientific Revolutions*, 3rd ed. (Chicago: University of Chicago Press, 1962, 1996), 151.

36 Ibid., 140.

37 Daniel Yankelovich, *The Magic of Dialogue: Transforming Conflict into Cooperation* (New York: Simon & Schuster, 1999), 12.

38 Exact source not known. I am indebted to David Beatty for the approximate words, attributed to Warren Buffett. The idea and language are consistent with many of Buffett's other quotable quotes. See, for example, "Words of Wisdom from Warren Buffet," *Forbes*, 10 January 2007: https://www.forbes.com/2007/01/10/leadership

-managing-money-lead-manage-cx_hc_0110buffett.html#2faa2a26438e, among many sources.

39 Michiyo Nakamoto and David Wighton, "Citigroup Chief Stays Bullish on Buy-Outs," *Financial Times*, 9 July 2007.

40 Lafley and Martin, *Playing to Win*, 206.

41 Rik Kirkland, "GE's Jeff Immelt on Evolving a Corporate Giant," *McKinsey Quarterly*, June 2015. https://www.mckinsey.com/business -functions/organization/our-insights/ges-jeff-immelt-on-evolving-a -corporate-giant.

42 Edgar H. Schein, *Organizational Culture and Leadership*, 5th ed. (Hoboken, NJ: John Wiley & Sons, 2017).

43 David Beatty, "Shareholder Activism: This Changes Everything," in *Rotman Management*, Winter 2017, 11. https://issuu.com/rotmanmag /docs/winter_17.

44 Dominic Barton, "Capitalism for the Long Term," *Harvard Business Review*, March 2011. https://hbr.org/2011/03/capitalism-for-the-long -term.

3. When Seeing Is Not Believing

1 McKinsey & Company, "The Four Global Forces Breaking All the Trends," April 2015. https://www.mckinsey.com/business-functions /strategy-and-corporate-finance/our-insights/the-four-global-forces -breaking-all-the-trends.

2 CNN, "M-Pesa: Kenya's Mobile Money Success Story Turns 10," 24 February 2017. https://www.cnn.com/2017/02/21/africa/mpesa -10th-anniversary/index.html.

3 Clayton M. Christensen, Michael Raynor, and Rory McDonald, "What Is Disruptive Innovation?" *Harvard Business Review*, December 2015, 6.

4 Ibid., 9.

5 "Tech's Raid on the Banks," *The Economist*, 4 May 2019.

6 Joseph Schumpeter, *Capitalism, Socialism and Democracy* (London: Routledge, 1942), 83.

7 In *The Theory of Economic Development* (1934), Joseph Schumpeter describes the evolution of complex business systems. Substantial research now supports this model of creative destruction. See Philippe

Aghion and Peter Howitt, "A Model of Growth through Creative Destruction," *Econometrica*, 60, 2 (1992): 323–51.

8 For the past fifteen years, the Institutions, Organizations and Growth Program (previously the Economic Growth and Policy Program) of the Canadian Institute for Advanced Research has focused on these issues. They have produced two books, *General Purpose Technologies and Economic Growth*, 1998, and *Institutions and Economic Performance*, 2008, both edited by Elthanan Helpman (Cambridge, MA: MIT Press).

9 Frances Westley, Brenda Zimmerman, and Michael Quinn Patton, in *Getting to Maybe: How the World Is Changed* (Toronto: Random House Canada, 2006), 66, point out that the pattern Schumpeter saw in economies, Holling, a conceptual founder of ecological economics, saw in natural ecosystems:

> The adaptive cycle tells us that unless we release the resources of time, energy, money and skill locked up in our routines and our institutions on a regular basis, it is hard to create anything new or to look at things from a different perspective. Without those perspectives, and the continuous infusion of novelty and innovation in our lives, our organizations and our systems, there is a slow but definite loss of resilience, and an increase in rigidity.
>
> Holling began his work in resilience by looking at ecosystems, particularly forests. He was fascinated by how often forests that had existed for hundreds of years went through massive change. Protecting them from fires, disease or drought was no way to guarantee their continued existence. Rather, forests seemed to use these massive changes as part of their ongoing evolution.

10 Helpman, ed., *General Purpose Technologies and Economic Growth*, 5.

11 Aghion and Howitt, "A Model of Growth through Creative Destruction."

12 Peter Howitt, "Measurement, Obsolescence and General Purpose Technologies," in Helpman, ed., *General Purpose Technologies and Economic Growth*, 219–51.

13 Philippe Aghion and Peter Howitt, "On the Macroeconomic Effects of Major Technological Change," in Helpman, ed., *General Purpose Technologies and Economic Growth*, 128.

14 The Economist Intelligence Unit, "Capital Markets in 2030: The
    Future of Equity Capital Markets," a PwC report. https://www.pwc
    .com/gx/en/audit-services/capital-market/publications/capital
    -markets-2030.pdf. Accessed 10 December 2019.

15 Salim Ismail, *Exponential Organizations* (New York: Diversion Books,
    2014), 25–35.

16 Peter H. Diamandis and Steven Kotler, *Abundance: The Future Is Better
    Than You Think* (New York: Free Press, 2014), 35.

17 "The Economics of Artificial Intelligence," *McKinsey Quarterly*, April
    2018. https://www.mckinsey.com/business-functions/mckinsey
    -analytics/our-insights/the-economics-of-artificial-intelligence.

18 Thomas S. Kuhn, *The Theory of Scientific Revolutions*, 3rd ed. (Chicago:
    The University of Chicago Press, 1962, 1996). Kuhn made several notable
    claims concerning the progress of scientific knowledge: that scientific fields
    undergo periodic "paradigm shifts" rather than solely progressing in a
    linear and continuous way, and that these paradigm shifts open up new
    approaches to understanding what scientists would never have considered
    valid before; and that the notion of scientific truth, at any given moment,
    cannot be established solely by objective criteria but is defined by a
    consensus of a scientific community. Competing paradigms are frequently
    incommensurable; that is, they are competing and irreconcilable accounts
    of reality. Thus, our comprehension of science can never rely wholly upon
    "objectivity" alone. Science must account for subjective perspectives as
    well, since all objective conclusions are ultimately founded upon the
    subjective conditioning/worldview of researchers and participants.

19 Ibid., 116.

20 Sir Arthur Conan Doyle, *The Adventures and Memoirs of Sherlock Holmes*
    (New York: Sterling Publishing, 2004), 309.

21 Peter L. Bernstein, *Against the Gods: The Remarkable Story of Risk* (New
    York: John Wiley & Sons, 1998), 329.

22 Summarized from the Preface to William Strauss and Neil Howe,
    Generations: The History of America's Future (New York: Broadway
    Books, 1991).

23 William Strauss and Neil Howe, *The Fourth Turning: What the Cycles of
    History Tell Us about America's Next Rendezvous with Destiny* (New York:
    Broadway Books, 1997), 6.

24 Brenda Zimmerman, *Edgeware – Primer and Principles*, 2000. Adapted from Brenda Zimmerman, Curt Lindberg, and Paul Plsek, *Edgeware: Lessons from Complexity Science for Health Care Leaders* (Dallas, TX: VHA Inc., 1998).

25 J. Schumpeter, *Capitalism, Socialism and Democracy* (New York: Harper and Brothers, 1942), 84.

26 A.D. Meyer, "Adapting to Environmental Jolts," *Administrative Science Quarterly*, 27 (1982): 515–37.

27 W. Erhard, M.C. Jensen, and S. Zaffron, "The Ontological Constraints Limiting Access to Leadership," *Harvard Business School Negotiation, Organizations and Markets Research Papers*, No. 09–022, 2008.

28 K.E. Weick, "Mundane Poetics: Searching for Wisdom in Organization Studies," *Organization Studies*, 25 (2004): 665.

29 S. Finkelstein, *Why Smart Executives Fail: And What You Can Learn from Their Mistakes* (New York: Penguin Publishing, 2009), 203.

30 A. Campbell, J. Whitehead, and S. Finkelstein, "Why Good Leaders Make Bad Decisions," *Harvard Business Review*, February 2009, 63.

31 Christopher Chabris and Daniel Simons, *The Invisible Gorilla: And Other Ways Our Intuitions Deceive Us* (New York: Crown, 2010). http://www.theinvisiblegorilla.com/gorilla_experiment.html. Accessed 10 December 2019.

32 Atul Gawande, "Annals of Medicine: The Itch – Its Mysterious Power May Be a Clue to a New Theory about Brains and Bodies," *The New Yorker*, 30 June 2008. https://www.newyorker.com/magazine/2008/06/30/the-itch.

33 J. Hawkins, *On Intelligence: How a New Understanding of the Brain Will Lead to the Creation of Truly Intelligent Machines* (New York: Times Books, 2004), 69.

34 Ibid.

35 Although Yousef Taleb, author of *The Black Swan* (New York: Random House, 2007), does not claim to have predicted the 2008 financial meltdown, he did identify one of its casualties: "As if we did not have enough problems, banks are now more vulnerable to the Black Swan and the ludic fallacy than ever before with 'scientists' among their staff taking care of exposures. The giant firm J.P. Morgan put the entire world at risk by introducing in the nineties RiskMetrics,

a phony method aiming at managing people's risks, causing the generalized use of the ludic fallacy, and bringing Dr. John's into power in place of the skeptical Fat Tonys. (A related method called 'Value-at-Risk,' which relies on the quantitative measurement of risk, has been spreading.) Likewise, the government sponsored institution, Fanny Mae, when I look at their risks, seems to be sitting on a barrel of dynamite, vulnerable to the slightest hiccup. But not to worry, their large staff of scientists deemed these events unlikely." In October 2008, Fanny Mae and its sister quasi-government agency, Freddie Mac, were taken over by the US government, part of the US$725 billion bailout.

4. Confronting Reality

1 Larry Bossidy and Ram Charan, *Execution: The Discipline of Getting Things Done* (New York: Crown Business, 2009), 7.
2 James S. Williams, "Thinking about Thinking," *Anomaly*, Williams Inference Service, Longmeadow, MA, 2002.
3 Ian Austen, "Research In Motion Eyes a Rebound," *New York Times*, 10 April, 2011. https://www.nytimes.com/2011/04/11/technology /companies/11rim.html.
4 Jaquie McNish and Sean Silcoff, *Losing the Signal: The Spectacular Rise and Fall of Blackberry* (Toronto: HarperCollins, 2015), 144.
5 Ibid., 145.
6 http://rnewswire.com/news-releases/blackberry-reports-fiscal -fourth-quarter-and-fiscal-year-2020-results-301032848.html. Accessed on 8 June 2020.
7 Dan Western, "30 Inspirational Charles Darwin Quotes," *Wealthy Gorilla*. https://wealthygorilla.com/charles-darwin-quotes/. Accessed 24 April 2019.
8 Peter M. Senge, *The Fifth Discipline: The Art & Practice of the Learning Organization* (London: Century Business, 1990), 4.
9 Arie P. de Geus, "Planning as Learning," *Harvard Business Review*, March-April 1988, 6. See also, Arie P. de Geus, *The Living Company: Habits for Survival in a Turbulent Business Environment* (Boston: Harvard Business School Press, 2002).

10 PwC Governance Insights Center, "PwC's 2019 Annual Corporate Directors Survey." https://www.pwc.com/us/en/services /governance-insights-center/assets/pwc-2019-annual-corporate -directors-survey-full-report-v2.pdf.pdf.

11 Edgar H. Schein with Peter Schein, *Organizational Culture and Leadership*, 5th ed. (Hoboken, NJ: John Wiley & Sons, 2017).

12 Ibid., 250.

13 Senge, *The Fifth Discipline*. According to Senge there are five disciplines necessary to create a learning organization – systems thinking, personal mastery, mental models, building shared vision, and team learning.

14 E.R. Auster, K.K. Wylie, and M.S. Valente, *Strategic Organizational Change: Building Change Capabilities in Your Organization* (New York: Palgrave MacMillan, 2005).

15 P. Smith, "The Learning Organization Ten Years On: A Case Study," *The Learning Organization*, 6, 5 (1999): 217–23.

16 D.A. Garvin, A.C. Edmondson, and F. Gino, "Is Yours a Learning Organization?" *Harvard Business Review*, March 2008. https://hbr .org/2008/03/is-yours-a-learning-organization.

17 R.W. Revans, "The Enterprise as a Learning System," *The Origins and Growth of Action Learning* (Bromley: Chartwell-Bratt, 1982), 281–6.

18 Michael C. Jensen, "Self-interest, Altruism, Incentives, and Agency Theory," *Journal of Applied Corporate Finance* (Summer 1994): 44.

19 W. Erhardt, M.C. Jensen, and S. Zaffron, "The Ontological Constraints Limiting Access to Leadership," *Harvard Business School Negotiation, Organizations and Markets Research Papers*, No. 09–022, 2008.

20 Roger Martin, *The Responsibility Virus: How Control Freaks, Shrinking Violets – and the Rest of Us – Can Harness the Power of True Partnership* (New York: Basic Books, 2002), 117.

21 Ibid., chapter 7, 105–29.

22 Chris Argyris, *Flawed Advice and the Management Trap* (New York: Oxford University Press, 2000).

23 Chris Argyris, "Teaching Smart People How to Learn," *Harvard Business Review*, May-June 1991, 5–15.

24 John P. Kotter, "Leading Change: Why Transformation Efforts Fail," *Harvard Business Review*, March-April 1995.

25 Thomas S. Kuhn, *The Structure of Scientific Revolutions*, 3rd ed. (Chicago: University of Chicago Press, 1962), 52.

26 Nate Silver, *The Signal and the Noise: Why So Many Predictions Fail – But Some Don't* (New York: Penguin Press, 2012).

27 G.S. Day and P.J. Shoemaker, "Scanning the Periphery," *Harvard Business Review* November 2005, 135.

28 Argyris, *Flawed Advice and the Management Trap*.

29 Michael J. Kami, *Trigger Points: How to Make Decisions Three Times Faster, Innovate Smarter, and Beat Your Competition by Ten Percent (It Ain't Easy!)* (New York: McGraw Hill, 1988), 147–51.

30 Williams, "Thinking about Thinking," *Anomaly*, Williams Inference Service, Longmeadow, MA, 2004.

31 Williams, "Thinking about Thinking," *Anomaly*, Williams Inference Service, Longmeadow, MA, 1996.

32 Thomas C. Schelling, *The Strategy of Conflict* (Boston: Harvard University Press, 1960, 1980), vi.

33 Wikipedia, "There Are Known Knowns." https://en.wikipedia .org/wiki/There_are_known_knowns#:~:text=Rumsfeld %20stated%3A,things%20we%20do%20not%20know. Accessed on 8 June 2020.

34 Steven A. Rosell, *Changing Frames: Leadership and Governance in the Information Age* (San Rafael, CA: Viewpoint Learning, 2000), 10.

35 Daniel Yankelovich, *The Magic of Dialogue: Transforming Conflict into Cooperation* (New York: Simon & Schuster, 1999), 16.

36 George Bernard Shaw, *Everybody's Political What's What* (London: Constable, 1944), Chapter 37, "Creed and Conduct," 330. https:// www.brainyquote.com/quotes/george_bernard_shaw_386923#: ~:text=Progress%20is%20impossible%20without%20change,their%20 minds%20cannot%20change%20anything.

5. What Boards Should Do, but Likely Won't

1 Yilmaz Arguden, *Boardroom Secrets: Corporate Governance for Quality of Life* (Basingstoke, Hants: Palgrave Macmillan, 2009), 1.

2 Michael C. Jensen, "The Modern Industrial Revolution, Exit and the Failure of Control Systems," *The Journal of Finance*, 48 (1993): 831.

3 Peter F. Drucker, *Management Challenges for the 21st Century* (New York: Harper Business Books, 1999), 53.

4 For example, K.R. Harrigan, "Exit Decisions in Mature Industries," *Academy of Management Journal*, 25 (1982): 707–32.

5 Jack Welch with John A. Byrne, *Jack: Straight from the Gut* (New York: Warner Business Books, 2001), 105.

6 It is interesting to note that this was the only speech that Jack Welch included in his book, *Jack: Straight from the Gut*, about his tenure as CEO of GE. This speech was important because it reflected his vision and strategic direction for the next twenty years. See Appendix A, pages 447 to 451.

7 Jay Dial and Kevin J. Murphy, "Incentives, Downsizing, and Value Creation at General Dynamics," *Journal of Financial Economics*, 37 (1995): 261–314.

8 Ibid.

9 Elizabeth Church, "The Gentle Magnate," *Globe and Mail*, 13 June 2006.

10 Until 1989, the Thomson organization included two public companies: Thomson Newspapers, headquartered in Toronto, Canada; and International Thomson, headquartered in London, United Kingdom. In 1989, the two companies were merged into the Thomson Corporation.

11 Jensen, "The Modern Industrial Revolution, Exit and the Failure of Control Systems," 831–80.

12 Martin Lipton and Jay W. Lorsch, "A Modest Proposal for Improved Corporate Governance," *The Business Lawyer*, 48, 1 (November 1992), 64.

13 Robert Monks and Nell Minow, *Corporate Governance*, 5th ed. (New York: John Wiley & Sons, 2011), 301.

14 Michael C. Jensen and William H. Meckling, "Theory of the Firm: Managerial Behavior, Agency Costs and Ownership Structure," *Journal of Financial Economics*, 3, 4 (October 1976): 305–60.

15 Jensen, "The Modern Industrial Revolution, Exit and the Failure of Control Systems," 849.

16 Dial and Murphy, "Incentives, Downsizing, and Value Creation at General Dynamics," 297.

17 Many public companies have been extending the terms for stock-related compensation to ten years.

6. Barbarians at the Gates

1 David Beatty, "Shareholder Activism: This Changes Everything,"
   Rotman Management, Winter 2017, 11. https://issuu.com/rotmanmag
   /docs/winter_17.
2 Michael C. Jensen, "Eclipse of the Public Corporation," *Harvard
   Business Review*, September-October 1989, 62.
3 Discussion with Mark Wiseman, CEO of Canada Pension Plan
   Investment Board, in March 2013.
4 Matt Fullbrook, "The Long-Term Survival of Family Business,"
   Clarkson Centre for Board Effectiveness, Rotman School of
   Management, University of Toronto, April 2018. Research
   paper. https://www.rotman.utoronto.ca/FacultyAndResearch
   /ResearchCentres/JohnstonCentre/Publications-and-surveys.
5 Antonio Spizzirri and Matt Fullbrook, "The Impact of Family Control
   on the Share Price Performance of Large Canadian Publicly Listed
   Firms (1998–2012)," Rotman School of Management, University of
   Toronto, June 2013. Research paper. https://www.rotman.utoronto
   .ca/FacultyAndResearch/ResearchCentres/JohnstonCentre
   /Publications-and-surveys/FamilyBusinessCorporateGovernance
   /Family-Firm-Performance-Study-June-2013.
6 Joseph Cyriac, Ruth De Backer, and Justin Sanders, "Preparing
   for Bigger, Bolder Shareholder Activists," *McKinsey Quarterly*,
   March 2014.
7 L.A. Bebchuk, A. Brav, & W. Jiang, "The Long-Term Effects of Hedge
   Fund Activism," *Columbia Law Review*, 115, 5 (June 2015): 1085–1155.
8 Jeff Immelt, "Keynote Address," Minds + Machines Conference,
   November 2012. https://www.youtube.com/watch?v=SvI3Pmv-DhE.
9 "Creation of GE Digital," *GE Newsroom*, 14 September 2015.
10 James Detar, "GE Sees Digital Revenue More Than Doubling to $15
   Billion by 2020," *Investor's Business Daily*, 23 June 2016.
11 GE, "GE Plans to Reduce Quarterly Dividend in Conjunction with
   Revised Capital Allocation Framework." Press release, 13 November
   2017. https://www.ge.com/news/press-releases/ge-plans-reduce
   -quarterly-dividend-conjunction-revised-capital-allocation-framework.
   Accessed 8 June 2020.

12 Yvan Allaire and Francois Dauphin, "A 'Successful' Case of Activism at the Canadian Pacific Railway," Harvard Law School Forum on Corporate Governance, 23 December 2016. https://corpgov.law .harvard.edu/2016/12/23/a-successful-case-of-activism-at-the -canadian-pacific-railway-lessons-in-corporate-governance.

13 The gap in operating ratio between CP Rail and CN Rail had not always been as wide. In fact, CP Rail had a lower operating ratio than CN Rail during a period in the 1990s when CN Rail was a crown corporation. The gap eventually widened, reaching unprecedented levels during Fred Green's tenure (the last full year of operating ratios attributable to Green was in 2011).

14 Michael E. Porter, "From Competitive Advantage to Corporate Strategy," *Harvard Business Review*, May-June 1987. Also, several studies by McKinsey & Company.

15 A. Brav, W. Jiang, S. Ma, & X. Tian, "How Does Hedge Fund Activism Reshape Corporate Innovation?" *Journal of Financial Economics*, 130, 2 (November 2018): 237–64. https://www.sciencedirect.com/science /article/abs/pii/S0304405X18301727.

16 V. Monga, D. Benoit, and T. Francis, "As Activism Rises, U.S. Firms Spend More on Buybacks Than Factories," *The Wall Street Journal*, 26 May 2015.

7. Transformation: Easier Said Than Done

1 Chris Zook and James Allen, *The Founder's Mentality: How to Overcome the Predictable Crises of Growth* (Boston: Harvard Business Review Press, 2016), 25–52.

2 Clayton M. Christensen, Thomas Bartman, and Derek Van Bever, "The Hard Truth about Business Model Innovation," *MIT Sloan Management Review* (Fall 2016): 31–40.

3 These observations support Joseph Schumpeter's *Theory of Economic Development* (1909/1934) discussed in chapter 3. They are also consistent with Michael Porter's descriptions of competitive advantage, whereby companies win by creating an interconnected activity system that is difficult to imitate or to change.

4 Larry Bossidy and Ram Charan, "Chapter 9: Seizing Opportunity: How the Thomson Corporation Transformed Itself," in *Confronting Reality: Doing What Matters to Get Things Right* (New York: Crown Publishing, 2004).

5 Ibid, 155–8.

6 Transcribed interviews with John Tory and Geoff Beattie, 6 May 2005. Author's notes from discussion with Ken Thomson on the same date.

7 Thomson Newspapers and International Thomson were separate public companies that were merged to create The Thomson Corporation in 1989.

8 Jay Dial and Kevin J. Murphy, "Incentives, Downsizing, and Value Creation at General Dynamics," *Journal of Financial Economics*, 37, 3 (March 1995): 261–314.

9 https://en.wikipedia.org/wiki/History_of_IBM, Accessed 8 June 2020.

10 Alexander S. Haslam, Stephen D. Reicher, and Michael J. Platow, *The New Psychology of Leadership: Identity, Influence and Power* (New York: Psychology Press, 2011), 199.

11 Ibid., 129.

12 Ibid., 206.

13 Harlan Cleveland, "The Twilight of Hierarchy: Speculation on the Global Information Society," *Public Administration Review*, 45, 1 (January-February 1985), 185.

14 George Bernard Shaw, *Everybody's Political What's What* (London: Constable, 1944), Chapter 37, "Creed and Conduct," 330. https://www.brainyquote.com/quotes/george_bernard_shaw_386923#:~:text=Progress%20is%20impossible%20without%20change,their%20minds%20cannot%20change%20anything. See chapter 4, note 36.

8. The Information Age Changes Everything

1 Based on concepts in Carlota Perez, *The Financial Crisis and the Future of Innovation: A View of Technical Change with the Aid of History* (Tallinn, Estonia: Technological University of Tallinn, February 2010).

2 Klaus Schwab, *The Fourth Industrial Revolution* (New York: Crown Business Publishing, 2016).

3 Internet World Stats, "Internet Usage Statistics: The Internet Big Picture," 3 March 2020. https://www.internetworldstats.com/stats.htm.

4 Bankmycell, "How Many Smartphones Are in the World? May 2020 Mobile User Statistics," May 2020. https://www.bankmycell.com /blog/how-many-phones-are-in-the-world.

5 Peter Diamandis and Steven Kotler, *Abundance: The Future Is Better Than You Think* (New York: Free Press, 2012).

6 Peter F. Drucker, *Management Challenges for the 21st Century* (New York: Harper Business Books, 1999), 102.

7 Niall Ferguson, *The Square and the Tower: Networks and Power from the Freemasons to Facebook* (New York: Penguin, 2018), 82–9.

8 Patricia Meredith, Steven A. Rosell, and Ged R. Davis, *Catalytic Governance: Leading Change in the Information Age* (Toronto: University of Toronto Press, 2016), 15.

9 Ocean Tomo, "Intangible Asset Market Value Study," 2017. www.oceantomo.com/intangible-asset-market-value-study/.

10 Jonathan Haskel and Stian Westlake, *Capitalism without Capital: The Rise of the Intangible Economy* (Princeton, NJ: Princeton University Press, 2018).

11 Rohinton P. Medhora, "Rethinking Policy in a Digital World," *Centre for International Governance Innovation*, Policy Brief No. 143 (November 2018): 2–3.

12 Peter Drucker, *Managing in Turbulent Times* (New York: Harper & Row, 1980).

13 Harlan Cleveland, "The Twilight of Hierarchy: Speculations on the Global Information Society," *Public Administration Review*, 45, 1 (January-February 1985): 185–6.

14 Ibid.

15 Salim Ismail, *Exponential Organizations* (New York: Division Books, 2014), 18–20.

16 Trefis Team, "As a Rare Profitable Unicorn, Airbnb Appears to Be Worth at Least $38 Billion," 11 May 2018. https://www.forbes.com /sites/greatspeculations/2018/05/11/as-a-rare-profitable-unicorn -airbnb-appears-to-be-worth-at-least-38-billion/#2f5402572741.

17 Social technology is a way of using human, intellectual, and digital resources in order to influence social processes. Examples are social software (e.g., wikis, blogs, social networks) and communication capabilities (e.g., Web conferencing) that are targeted at and enable social interactions.

18 Edgar H. Schein, *Organizational Culture and Leadership*, 5th ed. (Hoboken, NJ: John Wiley & Sons, 2017), 344.

19 Drucker, *Management Challenges for the 21st Century*, 92.

20 "The Rise of the Superstars," *The Economist*, 15 September 2016.

9. A New Governance Model

1 Business Roundtable, "Business Roundtable Redefines the Purpose of a Corporation to Promote 'An Economy That Serves All Americans,'" 19 August 2019. https://www.businessroundtable.org/business -roundtable-redefines-the-purpose-of-a-corporation-to-promote-an -economy-that-serves-all-americans.

2 Jay A. Conger, Edward E. Lawler III, and David L. Finegold, *Corporate Boards: New Strategies for Adding Value at the Top* (San Francisco: Jossey-Bass, 2001), 123.

3 Mark Bonchek, "From Gutenberg to Zuckerberg: The Transformation of Business," *Techonomy.com*, 1 October 2016.

4 Transcript of Zuckerberg interview, "In Conversation with Mark Zuckerberg," during the 2016 Techonomy Conference, 10 November 2016. Transcript posted on 17 November 2016. http://techonomy .com/conf/te16/videos-conversations-with-2/in-conversation-with -mark-zuckerberg/. Accessed 8 June 2020.

5 Ibid.

6 Sam Biddle, "Facebook, I'm Begging You, Please Make Yourself Better," *The Intercept*, 10 November 2016. https://theintercept .com/2016/11/10/facebook-im-begging-you-please-make-yourself -better/. Accessed 8 June 2020.

7 "The Antisocial Network: Facebook and Democracy," *The Economist*, 24 March 2018.

8 "Facebook's Third Act," *The Economist*, 7 March 2019.

9 Chris Zook and James Allen, *The Founder's Mentality: How to Overcome the Predictable Crises of Growth* (Boston: Harvard Business Review Press, 2016), 130.

10 Clayton M. Christensen, Thomas Bartman, and Dereck van Bever, "The Hard Truth about Business Model Innovation," *Sloan Management Review* (Fall 2016): 32.

11 In 2019, 35 per cent of all new companies listed on the TSX had dual share structures.

12 Matthew Merkley, "Multiple Voting Shares: Don't Call It a Comeback," Blake, Cassels & Graydon, LLP, online, 9 February 2015. https://www.blakes.com/English/Resources/TrendsInsights/Pages/details.aspx?AnnouncementID=78. Accessed 15 June 2019.

13 Matt Fullbrook, "The Long-Term Survival of Family Business," Clarkson Centre for Board Effectiveness, Rotman School of Management, University of Toronto, April 2018. Research paper. https://www.rotman.utoronto.ca/FacultyAndResearch/ResearchCentres/JohnstonCentre/Publications-and-surveys.

14 Edgar H. Schein with Peter Schein, *Organizational Culture and Leadership*, 5th ed. (Hoboken, NJ: John Wiley & Sons, 2017), 343.

15 The form of dialogue was developed by Steven Rosell, Daniel Yankelovich, and their colleagues at Viewpoint Learning and applied to a wide range of issues in the United States and Canada, including fiscal policy, health care, education, climate change, and sustainability.

16 Peter F. Drucker, *Management Challenges for the 21st Century* (New York: Harper Business, 1999), 110.

17 Joe Lukomnik, "Will Accountants Become the Weavers of the 21st Century?" *Accounting Today*, 19 November 2018. https://www.accountingtoday.com/opinion/will-accountants-become-the-weavers-of-the-21st-century.

18 Warren E. Buffett, "Letter to the Shareholders," *Berkshire Hathaway 2018 Annual Report*, 23 February 2019, 3. https://www.berkshirehathaway.com/letters/2018ltr.pdf. Accessed 8 June 2020.

19 Mark Bonchek and Barry Libert, "To Build Your Platform Network Your Capital," *Harvard Business Review*, 14 July 2017.

20 Drucker, *Management Challenges for the 21st Century*, 122–3.

21 Michael C. Jensen, "Eclipse of the Public Corporation," *Harvard Business Review*, September-October 1989.

22 Institute of Corporate Directors, "Deft Governance," *Director Journal*, September-October 2015.

23 Schein and Schein, *Organizational Culture and Leadership*, 348.

24 Dominic Barton and Mark Wiseman, "Where Boards Fall Short," *Harvard Business Review*, January-February 2015.

Index